Parenting
After
Divorce

RebuildingBooks®
Relationships – Divorce – and Beyond

Parenting
After
Divorce

*Resolving Conflicts and
Meeting Your Children's Needs*

SECOND EDITION

Philip M. Stahl, Ph.D.

Impact **Publishers**®
ATASCADERO, CALIFORNIA

Copyright © 2000, 2007
Philip M. Stahl, Ph.D.
First Edition, 2000
Second Edition, 2007
First Printing, October 2007

ATTENTION ORGANIZATIONS AND CORPORATIONS:
This book is available at quantity discounts on bulk purchases for educational, business, or sales promotional use. For further information, please contact Impact Publishers, P.O. Box 6016, Atascadero, CA 93423-6016, Phone: 1-800-246-7228, e-mail: sales@impactpublishers.com

Library of Congress Cataloging-in-Publication Data

Stahl, Philip Michael.
    Parenting after divorce : resolving conflicts and meeting your children's needs / Philip M. Stahl. — 2nd ed.
        p. cm. — (Rebuilding books)
    Includes bibliographical references and index.
    ISBN-13: 978-1-886230-84-2 (alk. paper)
    1. Children of divorced parents. 2. Parenting. 3. Divorced parents—Psychology.
4. Divorce—Psychological aspects. I. Title.
    HQ777.5.S72 2007
    306.89—dc22

                                                                            2007026834

Publisher's Note
This publication is designed to provide accurate and authoritative information in regard to the subject matter covered. It is sold with the understanding that the publisher is not engaged in rendering psychological, legal, or other professional services. If expert assistance or counseling is needed, the services of a competent professional should be sought.

Impact Publishers and colophon are registered trademarks of Impact Publishers, Inc.

Cover design by Gayle Downs, Gayle Force Design, Atascadero, California
Author photo © Marvin Moore Photography
Composition by UB Communications, Parsippany, New Jersey
Printed in the United States of America on recycled, acid-free paper.
Published by **Impact** 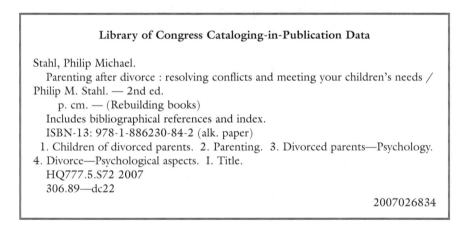 **Publishers**®
POST OFFICE BOX 6016
ATASCADERO, CALIFORNIA 93423-6016
www.impactpublishers.com

To the children of divorce.

Contents

Preface

I'VE SPENT THE LAST TWENTY-FIVE YEARS of my professional life working with children and families of divorce. In more recent years, it has become a near-exclusive practice, as I have been a therapist, child custody evaluator, mediator, parenting coordinator, researcher, author, and trainer in the field. I have actively participated with the Association of Family and Conciliation Courts (AFCC) and the American Psychological Association (APA) and local interdisciplinary committees of professionals in trying to promote a better understanding of how divorce affects children and families and to learn what parents can do to help their children adjust in a healthier way to divorce. I have also been teaching judges about various aspects of high-conflict divorce, at statewide judicial education conferences and with the National Judicial College and the National Council of Juvenile and Family Court Judges. This book, meant for the parents of divorce, is an outgrowth of that work.

I am also a divorced father and bring a personal perspective to my professional life. I have shared custody of my children, and I've tried to follow the guidelines I encourage in this book. In both my personal and professional life, I have seen what works, and what doesn't. Like all parents, I have made mistakes and tried to learn from them. Finally, I have talked with my own children about my professional and personal observations, as well as their feelings and experiences.

In this book, I have tried to provide you, the reader, with a different perspective on divorce. *Your divorce doesn't have to damage your children*, especially if you take the time and effort to be a responsible parent and limit your children's exposure to your conflicts. I know that most parents want to raise their children in an emotionally healthy way, and I'm confident that you will find my suggestions and insights helpful.

I have also learned a lot from children over the years. The effects of divorce on children can be many or few, depending on how parents handle things. Usually, parents argue a lot before getting a divorce. If they continue arguing after the divorce, their children are likely to suffer. If parents learn to settle their differences and become more content and happier after the divorce, they can usually do a more effective job of parenting. Their children will be more likely to adjust well. In this book, I will share observations from many children, and from adults — some now divorced — who were children when their own parents divorced. You'll find some of their comments throughout the book, others in an entire chapter devoted to the words of children. If you learn from their words, as I have, you can help your own children.

Notes on Gender Neutrality. I've tried to write this book in a gender-neutral way. I don't like to use the phrases "he/she" or "s/he" that are sometimes used in books. In my examples, I might write about a parent, and say "he" did something. At other times, I might say "she" did something. Sometimes these actions are negative and sometimes they are positive. I recognize that all parents, both mothers and fathers, are capable of poor parenting decisions and behaviors, and equally capable of healthy parenting decisions and behaviors. By alternating the pronouns that I use, I've tried to be sensitive to feelings in this area.

I also recognize that judges, attorneys, and mental health professionals are equally likely to be male or female. Again, by alternating the gender of the pronouns I use, I have tried to remain gender-neutral.

Along with this, I've written about some very difficult personality traits and behaviors that some parents, both mothers and fathers, experience. While studies suggest that men are more likely to be violent than women, parents of both genders can be physically or emotionally abusive to each other and their children. By balancing and alternating the genders in these examples, I have tried to remain gender-neutral.

Notes on Examples. Throughout the book, I have also provided many examples of families who engage in both healthy and unhealthy behaviors. All such examples are fictional, yet are based on real-life examples in my experience. Names and ages of the children have been changed, and circumstances have been modified. This helps to protect confidentiality of those with whom I have worked and also allows me to create examples to match a point I am trying to make.

Notes on Research. I refer many times in the book to "research" on divorce. There continues to be a growing and extensive body of literature in this area. Some of that research was generated by the time I wrote the first edition of this book, and considerable research has occurred in the past seven years. In a publication for professionals, I would provide readers with citations to research that I cite; since this book is for parents I'm not including the research references. However, I have included footnotes at the end of chapters in which there is some specific area of research that is particularly relevant. Additionally, you'll find a list of books and additional research listed in the Appendix that might benefit you. Finally, when an association, such as AFCC, has Model Standards of Practice, I am including a link to their current website for those model standards.

Notes of Appreciation. I would like to thank many people for their assistance in this project. First and foremost, I would like to thank the thousands of divorced children who have shared their touching experiences with me and taught me about their feelings. Not only has that helped me strive to be a better parent, but it has helped me in my work with other parents of divorce.

Second, I would like to thank the many parents of those children who have shared their frustrations and offered suggestions that have worked for them. I have shared many of their ideas and experiences with you in this book.

Third, I would like to thank the researchers and other professionals, including court professionals, attorneys, and judges, many of whom I have met through AFCC and APA or at local interdisciplinary meetings, who have helped all of us learn more about the effects of divorce on children. Some of these professionals are also divorced and have shared important perspectives for this project, as well. In particular, I would like to thank those who shared thoughts and comments about the original edition of this book, which have been included in the many changes I have made for this edition.

Fourth, I would like to thank Bob Alberti and the staff of Impact Publishers. Bob had the wisdom to see that this book is different than many of the other books on divorce and the willingness to encourage its success. Bringing a book from the idea stage to press is a difficult job and they have made this task easier with their assistance. The same has been true for this updated edition, as well.

Finally, I would like to thank my wife Ruth, and my children Jason and Rebecca. Not only have they supported and encouraged me to complete this project, but they have reviewed it and made countless suggestions on how to make this better. Ruth is an excellent organizer and she has helped me keep a sharp focus on the task. Jason has provided valuable insight into many of the complex issues affecting families, and he has excellent editorial skills. Rebecca has provided the perspective of a child who has experienced about half of her life with divorced parents. Currently finishing law school, she is thoughtful and has a keen sense of humor that helps me deal with difficult challenges. Their love and inspiration has helped me stay focused on the needs of all children, no matter what I do.

Maricopa County, Arizona
Summer 2007

Introduction

IN 2007, HIGH-CONFLICT DIVORCE received considerable publicity when actor Alec Baldwin's angry voice mail to his daughter was posted online. Baldwin had been upset that she was not available to take his phone call — something that reportedly happened many times since his divorce from Kim Basinger several years before. While such phone messages likely occur throughout the United States on a daily basis, this one made headlines around the world when someone posted the message on a celebrity website for the entire world to hear. Over the next several days, TV talk show hosts, comedians, and others expressed outrage about his behavior, though many also questioned who was responsible for putting this onto the web. Baldwin himself went on several TV talk shows, apologizing for his phone message, questioning why his daughter had not been available for regularly scheduled phone calls, and wanting to find out who put the phone message on the internet. He alleged that his daughter had been alienated against him by her mother.

While Alec Baldwin's anger and family problems gained the attention of celebrity watchers in the U.K., the United States and elsewhere, family conflicts of this type occur all of the time in everyday life around the world.

Among other examples from my experience, Jim and Kathy have been married for twelve years. They have three children: Johnny is eleven, Kirsten seven, and Brian four. Jim and Kathy no longer love one another; in fact, they rarely spend much time together at all. After years of arguing and drifting apart, they've decided to get a divorce. Like most divorcing parents, the only thing they can agree on is that they want their children to continue to grow up in a healthy environment. Kathy has been a stay-at-home mom, but will need to go back to work. She's worried about how her kids will adjust to daycare. Jim has worked full-time, been a coach to Johnny and Kirsten in soccer, and wants to stay active with the kids. Both of them are worried about money, and whether there will be enough to go around. Jim wants to share joint physical custody of the kids, but Kathy doesn't want the kids to have two homes. Kathy wants primary physical custody of the kids. Jim wasn't there very much and she's worried about how they will adjust to two homes — especially Brian, who seems sensitive and has never slept away from home. They get along reasonably well and agree on the basics for the kids. But they don't communicate very well and both of them worry about what their children need, especially since they are of such different ages.

Michael and Susan have been divorced for six years. Both are remarried. They have two children, Sara, age 14, and Kyle, age 10. They continue to argue over everything, even worse than when they were married. Sara is failing in school, experiments with drugs, and is "boy-crazy." Kyle has a learning disability and gets into fights at school. Both parents blame each other every time one of the children has a new problem. Michael has taken Susan to court five times in the six years since the divorce, claiming that she is an unfit parent, twice alleging that her new husband is abusive to the children. Susan has taken Michael to court four times in the six years, twice because of child support issues and twice because he refused to bring the children back to her care. Susan claims that his new wife forces the kids to call her "mom" and constantly criticizes her. They are constantly arguing over the parenting schedule, vacations, the children's extra-curricular activities, Sara's schoolwork, and Kyle's behavior. If they aren't arguing, they aren't talking at all. Both of them use the children as messengers so that they don't fight. The kids are sick of the conflict.

Mary and Dennis have never been married. They have one child, Erica, who is 18 months old. Dennis wants joint physical custody of Erica, since both of them work, and he thinks he's as good a parent as Mary. As the mother, Mary wants custody and wants to take Erica with her and to move back home to her parents, who live in Texas. She'll be willing to let Dennis come to Texas to visit with Erica when he is off of work. When Erica starts school, Mary figures Erica can visit her dad in the summers and at major holidays. Neither of them is thinking very much of how all of this will affect Erica. Since they never lived together, they don't trust each other. They have no idea how to share the parenting after they separate.

Raising Children of Divorce in a Healthy Way

The parents of over one million children become divorced each year. Now *you* are getting — or have already gone through — a divorce. Whether you've chosen to get a divorce or your partner is divorcing you, whether you're certain it's the right thing, or you're not sure about it, your most important task is to raise your children in the healthiest possible way.

If you are like many people getting a divorce, you've thought about it for years, but didn't get divorced because of fears about how it might affect your children. Regardless of your motivation or your willingness about the divorce, your divorce is likely to affect your children in many ways. While many children are upset by a divorce, especially at the beginning, you can help your children maintain a healthy adjustment in their lives.

Because Jim and Kathy don't argue much, their children may feel some relief. In fact, about twenty percent of divorcing parents will have much less conflict after separation. In contrast, Michael and Susan's kids are having a miserable time, since these parents are constantly in conflict. They don't know the danger signs related to Sara's school failure and drug use. Instead, they just continue to argue and blame each other.

Statistics suggest that about twenty percent of the parents who separate and divorce will have very high conflict for many years after the divorce. The courts try to provide services to help parents like this, but in truth, only the parents can make a true commitment to their children. Your ongoing commitment to your child's well-being is vital. Stay alert to signs of distress in your children. Don't pressure a child to choose sides between you and your ex-spouse. Understand your child's feelings and separate them from your own. This book is designed to help you with that process.

Children of Divorce Can Survive

Over the last twenty years, researchers have found that children of divorce go through a variety of responses to divorce. At first, children may experience sadness and confusion, and they may feel insecure and shaken. After all, their immediate world has been turned upside down. Many children feel responsible for the family break-up. Frequently, families move, incomes are reduced, and there is tremendous turmoil in their lives. This turmoil and change causes great stress for your children, in large part because they don't know what is going to happen to them. Parents, often caught up in their own turmoil, may not listen well to their children or help their kids understand what's going on.

Initially, most children want their family back together; and they typically feel sad about this loss in their life. Most of the divorce research shows that boys, in particular, have a very difficult time adjusting to the early stages of divorce, and are at risk for exhibiting increased problems in school, with peer relationships, and to authority. This same research shows that girls often become more withdrawn, but are likely to remain quieter about their internal response to the divorce. These problems are fairly typical in the first year of divorce, but parents can help their children over time in many ways. Let's take a look at four primary things parents must do to ensure their children a healthy adaptation to divorce:

• *Stay involved!* Research suggests that children do best when they have active contact with both of their parents. When parents divorced in the 1960's and 1970's, many children wished for the return of the marital unit. Among other reasons, this was at least partly because children experienced the actual loss of a parent who dropped out of their life. In more recent years, there's been a growing emphasis on joint custody and an encouragement for both parents to stay actively involved with their children. However, if Erica moves to Texas with her mother, she'll only see her dad once a month, maybe less. This will be a great loss to her. Erica will have lost any hope for a family unit, and for a stable and consistent relationship with her dad. Frequent and continuing contact with both of her parents would reduce the losses in Erica's life and help her to adjust more easily to her parents' separation.

• *Maintain continuity in your child's life!* Insecurity can be reduced and stability can be maintained after the divorce when you and your ex-spouse allow your children to continue the activities they enjoyed prior to your divorce. Johnny and Kirsten will be attending the same school, continuing in their music lessons and athletic interests, and don't have to make new friends. Their adjustment to their parents' divorce will be much easier.

• *Avoid conflict in front of your kids!* Continued research has shown that a significant factor affecting children's adjustment to divorce is the amount of conflict that continues between parents after the divorce, especially conflict to which the child is exposed. Sara and Kyle are both depressed and angry because their parents seem to hate each other more than they love the kids. You got divorced to end your relationship and move on in your life, but you can't do this if you stay stuck in substantial conflict about your children. When your conflicts continue, your child stays stuck in your turmoil. Children hate being in the middle of their parents' conflict and hate the battling going on around them. Children can't recover from the disruption of divorce if there is continued disruption because their parents stay in conflict with each other. The healthiest way for you to help your child after your divorce is to reduce your level of conflict and make an active effort to keep all of your conflict away from your children, no matter what.

- *Talk with your children!* Research suggests that the majority of parents don't tell their children much about the changes which are about to occur when parents get divorced. However, if you don't talk with them about what's going on, your children will be scared, confused, and overwhelmed. Talk with them about the custody and visitation arrangements, before you settle on them. Ask them what they're afraid of, and then reassure them. Let them know the divorce isn't their fault, and tell them what will — and what won't — change in their lives. Don't make promises you can't keep; that'll double their disappointment. They need to count on you for the truth and for their stability. It's important to help your children understand and navigate their way around their world and to help them understand and sort out their feelings. By talking with them honestly, by listening to their fears and worries, and by teaching them how to deal with their experiences, you can help prepare them. This is important for all parents, but even more so for parents as they go through divorce.

Forgiving: Getting Past Getting Dumped

Research has consistently shown that forgiveness is an important virtue that allows for healthier living. Over the years, I've found that one of the main reasons that a parent can't move on in life is because that parent can't forgive his ex-spouse. One of the reasons that Michael and Susan keep arguing is that neither can forgive the other for the many hurts over the years. Maybe you won't forgive your ex-spouse because she divorced you. Or because of how you were treated during your relationship. Ultimately, most divorced persons aren't able to forgive their ex-spouses because they are no longer loved. Until you learn to forgive, you will remain angry!

Unfortunately, following a divorce, this anger is likely to get expressed in front of your children. You don't want to hurt your children, but when this anger spills out and your children experience it, the fallout is damaging to them. Sometimes the anger is obvious, especially when you make derogatory statements about each other or argue with each other in front of your children. The anger might also be more subtle, such as when you tell your child that he doesn't have to listen to his other parent. I have known parents who get angry while reading a note from the other parent and say to their children, in exasperation, "Here! Read this and you'll know why I can't deal with your father." If you haven't learned to forgive, you will act in ways that will be damaging to your child, usually because you will be more focused on avenging your feelings than responding to your child and her feelings.

In contrast, if you can forgive your ex-spouse, you'll go a long way toward keeping your children out of the middle and model for them healthy skills of conflict resolution. If you have truly forgiven your ex-spouse, you will be able to communicate without arguing and bringing up problems of the past. You will be able to get past the "couple's conflict" and focus on the needs of your children. If you are a forgiving parent, you will say "hello" to the other parent in public places and act in a business-like way when issues need to be discussed. In essence, as forgiving parents, you will treat your ex-spouse just as you would treat other acquaintances and business partners. This is because, for all practical purposes, divorced parents who have forgiven one another are able to be partners in raising their children.

Maintaining Self-Responsibility

As a psychologist, I often hear complaints from divorced parents about their ex-spouses and how they are causing problems. I'll hear about the critical things the other parent says to children. I'll hear about the times the other parent interferes with their time with their children. I'll hear about the difficulty the other parent causes on the athletic fields when watching their child's events. It is quite rare, though refreshing, when parents come in and talk about their own difficulty in these same endeavors. Recently, a parent came into my office and said "We've both been acting like three-year-olds," and went on to elaborate that "all we ever fight about is petty things!"

To forgive and resolve conflicts, and take care of your children, you'll need to stop blaming your ex-spouse and focus on yourself and your own behavior. Realize that there is really only one person you can control: *yourself!* You are likely to get frustrated with your ex-spouse, and you might wish that his behavior was different. You might feel hurt and angry when the other parent acts in a way that you feel is damaging to your child. However, you can only control your own behavior, and you can only take responsibility for yourself. If you learn to separate your own behavior and your own relationship with your children from the other parent, and if each of you maintains self-responsibility, your children would grow up with less conflict in their lives and more inner peace.

Do Your Best, Regardless of the Other Parent

Since you can only be responsible for yourself, it's important to do your best, no matter what the other parent does. Suppose your ex-spouse tells your children that you were mean and abusive during the marriage. They are likely to feel bad, regardless of whether they agree with the statement. However, if you call her a liar and then tell your children that she ran off with her boyfriend, your children will feel even worse. This kind of "reciprocal name-calling" is too stressful for your children.

Instead, when your child tells you that your ex-spouse told her something bad about you, your best response is with the same emotion you would express if a schoolmate said something mean to your child. Tell the child that you understand she feels sad when her mom says mean things about you and ask her if she feels the same way. If her mom said you were mean, ask your daughter if *she* feels that you're mean. Thank her for telling you about her feelings, and let her know that you'll always be there to help her understand how she feels. Stay calm, just as you would if it weren't your ex-wife who said something mean to your daughter.

Similarly, if your ex starts fights at your child's school concert, and if you engage in the argument and get even louder in your name-calling, your child will probably withdraw and become depressed. He'll become embarrassed. (Wouldn't you?) However, by acting in a healthy way, regardless of the way your ex acts, you can ensure that your child will feel less tension — at least some of the time.

An unfortunate, though common, "game" among divorcing parents is "tit for tat." It seems that, no matter what one parent does, the other will do a little bit more just to get back or get even. Not only does this waste your energy and keep you embroiled in conflict, it is highly damaging to your children. When you hear from your child that your ex-spouse has called you some terrible names, it is important to speak gently to your child and tell him that the other parent is entitled to his opinion, but don't retaliate. Let your child know that it doesn't bother you what the other parent says, and that you won't do the same thing. You can help your child learn to relax and ignore those statements. By not retaliating, you can insure that your child will feel more relaxed and at peace when in your presence.

You obviously can't do anything to ease the pain or conflicts that your children feel when they see or hear damaging things from the other parent, but by doing your own individual best, and by taking responsibility for your own behavior and acting in your children's best interests regardless of the other parent's actions, you can help meet your children's need for peace.

Working Together for Your Child

The ultimate goal for divorced parents is to act in a mutually responsible way. If you are responsible, you will:

- avoid conflict in front of your child
- share appropriate information about your child with the other parent
- communicate about your child's developmental issues, school information, and other medical information
- work together as partners in raising your child

While minor day-to-day decisions will be made independent of the other parent, the healthiest situation will be when no major decision is made without consultation with the other parent. Before a child is enrolled in summer school, an art class, an athletic team, etc., both parents should discuss it and reach a mutually agreeable decision. When you take your child out of town on a vacation, you need to give emergency information to the other parent, and you will want to make certain that your child calls the other parent. While you are likely to want some privacy, it is important to balance your need for privacy with the need of your child to share information with whomever she wants, as well as the need for the other parent to reach your child in case of an emergency.

It is healthiest for your children when they see both of you attending their school conferences, both of you participating in their music concerts and athletic events, and both of you involved in their religious training and other pursuits. In essence, it is healthiest for your children when they see both of you actively participating in their lives, and when they know that both of you are actively involved in the decision-making on their behalf. When your children can see that their parents, who have stopped loving each other, still care enough to act in a responsible and healthy way, they will adjust more easily to your divorce. It helps your children to learn that you have forgiven your ex-spouse, you have chosen to reduce your role in the conflicts, and to get on with your life in healthy ways. Your child can learn from your behavior about forgiving others, as well. The peace that this engenders is the greatest gift you can give to your children as you work to help them learn and grow in their own life.

Summing Up

In this introduction, I have focused on the primary issues which help parents resolve their conflicts and meet their children's needs after a divorce. Once again, you can help children adjust to your divorce in a healthy way if you:

- Stay involved
- Maintain continuity in your child's life
- Forgive your ex-spouse
- Take self-responsibility
- Manage your conflicts away from your child
- Talk with your child
- Do your best parenting regardless of the other parent
- Work together in a mutually responsible way to meet your children's needs.

If you stop acting like children, end your petty arguing, and be personally self-responsible, your children can adjust more easily.

The Rest of the Book

The rest of this book will focus on many of these issues in greater detail in order to help you parent your children more effectively after your divorce.

Chapter 1 focuses on how conflict affects your children, and how the fighting may lead to irreparable harm. You will learn how to talk with your children in a healthy way, and how to ease your child's transitions between your homes, whether or not you share joint physical custody.

Chapters 2 and 3 teach you about the concept of sharing. You probably put a lot of effort into teaching your young children how to share; now it's time for you and your ex to learn how important it is to share your children with each other. You will be shown how to focus on your own relationship with your child and parent your children in a healthy way. You will learn the value of a parenting plan and how it may help reduce your conflict. You will also learn to recognize the benefits of supporting your child's relationship with your ex-spouse, while enhancing your own parent-child relationship, even if your time with your child is limited. You will learn to talk in a businesslike way with each other, even though you may not like your ex-spouse. Most important, you will learn the critical lesson that, when you go after a *win*, everyone, especially your children, *lose*. You will learn how to respond to your child's negative statements about the other parent and recognize that you must avoid conflicts in front of your children. You will learn to manage your conflicts in a healthier way, for the sake of your children.

Chapter 4 focuses on your child's developmental needs and how divorce affects them according to their age. You will be shown specific techniques for helping them with those age-appropriate needs.

Chapter 5 outlines a style of talking to your children. You will learn four basic principles in talking to your children. These include being honest, paying attention to your children's feelings, understanding what your children are really trying to say, and finally, helping them understand the concepts of divorce. You will also learn how to talk about the divorce over time, and consider various questions your children may ask according to their development.

Chapter 6 will help teach you that your children's activities, school life, social life, toys and clothes are theirs. You will learn to separate your feelings from those of your child and learn how to set up healthy boundaries in your parent-child relationship. Additionally, you will learn how to set up healthy boundaries in your relationship with your ex-spouse.

In chapter 7, you will learn how you can stop worrying about criticism from the other parent. You will learn that both of you have strengths and weaknesses, how to take self-responsibility, and avoid the trap of being more like a peer to your child. You will learn to discipline your child, without fear of his — or your ex-spouse's — blackmail, something that is quite common in divorce. Ultimately, you will learn the skills necessary to be yourself, and parent to the best of your own individual ability.

Chapter 8 will convince you that one of the most important tasks of parenting is *taking care of yourself.* Just like flight attendants on an airplane tell passengers to take care of themselves first in an emergency, and then take care of the child next to them, you will learn that, when you are clear within yourself, and can understand and manage your own emotions, you'll be better prepared to take care of your children. You will discover how to use your time away from your child to rediscover yourself. Most importantly, you will learn the skills to get over the loss of your marriage, and forgive your ex-spouse. In all of these ways, you will learn that the more you understand yourself, your own feelings, and your own needs, the more you will improve your job as a parent!

In chapter 9, you will learn about interventions that may help you when these other efforts fail. These include mediation, parent education, custody evaluation, the use of a co-parent counselor, and the potential use of a parenting coordinator when the conflicts persist. This chapter teaches you the benefits of using a system of binding arbitration to settle day-to-day issues, so that your children are not so negatively affected by your conflicts.

In chapter 10, you will be introduced to certain special problems and how to deal with them, including issues of alienation, domestic violence, difficult new partners, and dealing with a very difficult ex-spouse. Additionally, this chapter will focus heavily on ways in which specific personality traits often make it difficult for parents to cooperate and resolve differences in a healthier way.

Chapter 11 teaches effective ways to deal with the courts so that you can avoid damaging litigation. You will come to understand that adversaries always lose, and why working toward settlement should be your desired goal. This chapter will teach you to focus on your child's feelings and needs, not your parental rights. At the end of this chapter, you will learn about an alternative vision for courts that will discourage litigation as a means of solving family problems.

The final chapter (12) is written from the words of children. Statements made in therapy sessions, evaluation sessions, and special writings for this book will be used to pull together the main ideas in this book. While examples of children's comments are interspersed throughout the book, this chapter will highlight things that children like about the way their parents act, and things they wish their parents had done differently. In their own poignant words, children will describe what they like and don't like about how parents act regarding their divorce. They will point out how it feels to be victims and prisoners of "divorce wars." They will describe the parenting techniques that have been successful and helped them survive and grow, in spite of their parents' divorce. It is my hope that these words will provide you with the clearest example of what needs to change to help you resolve your conflicts and parent in a healthier way.

The appendix at the end will provide you with a sample list of books for you and your children. You'll also find examples of specific questions children ask, and how to respond to them. The last word offers specific techniques for troubleshooting conflicts with your ex-spouse.

As detailed as this book is, it is not a comprehensive text on parenting or child management. Nor is it focused on the divorce process itself and how to manage it. It is also not about co-parenting, though many concepts of co-parenting are included. I've listed many books on those topics in the appendix. Instead, this book is about parenting after divorce, how to take responsibility for your own behavior, and how to minimize the damage to your children.

Let me end this introduction with a comprehensive statement of rights that your children should expect from your divorce. While many parents go to court expecting to gain their rights, I believe that parents need to support their children's rights after a divorce. I encourage you to adopt these rights in your post-divorce life. If you do, your child's adjustment to your divorce will be significantly healthier.

Bill of Rights for Children Whose Parents Are Divorced

Children have the right to:

- Know the truth about your divorce, with simple explanations!
- Be protected from the parental warfare!
- Develop and maintain an independent relationship with each parent!
- Be free from having to take sides with, defend, or denigrate either parent!
- Be free of responsibility for having caused the divorce!
- Be reassured that they are not to blame!
- Be free from having to take over parental responsibilities! A child can't become the "man of the house" or the "little mother"!
- Expect that both parents will follow through with the parenting plan and honor specific commitments for scheduled time with their child!
- Expect that both parents will inform each other about medical, dental, education and legal matters concerning the child!
- Receive love, guidance, patience, understanding, and limits from their parents!
- Spend time with each parent, regardless of financial support!
- Be financially supported by both parents, regardless of how much time is spent with either parent!
- Maintain privacy when talking to either parent on the telephone!
- Have a personal sleeping area and space for possessions in each parent's home!
- Participate in age-appropriate activities so long as those activities do not significantly impair their relationship with either parent!
- Avoid being told the painful details of their parents' legal proceedings!
- Avoid being made to feel guilty for loving both parents!
- Avoid making the custody / visitation decisions!
- Avoid being cross-examined by one parent after spending time with the other parent!
- Not to be used as a messenger or spy between the parents!
- Not to be asked to keep secrets from the other parent!

CHAPTER 1

Conflict, Communication, Co-Parenting, and Competition

How Your Battles with Your Ex Affect Your Children

"A thing is not necessarily true because a man dies for it."
— Oscar Wilde

IN NEARLY THIRTY YEARS of work with families of divorce, I find that one of the hardest things for parents to do when they are angry or hurt is to put their differences aside for the sake of their children. Yet social science research tells us that children are most likely to adjust in healthy ways to their parents' divorce if they are able to put aside those differences.

Does this sound familiar?

> Sean and Maria argue all the time. They have five children, ages five to sixteen. They say terrible things about each other in front of the children. Maria quizzes the children about Sean's girlfriend after they spend time in Sean's house and refers to her as "the tramp." Whenever Sean calls to talk to the children, Maria hangs up the phone. When Sean picks the kids up from school for the weekend, he yells at them about what their mother has forgotten to send along. Maria has been known to keep their twelve-year-old daughter home from basketball practice because Sean would be there. The court doesn't allow both parents to attend the children's events at the same time since there have been so many arguments.

> The children are depressed and scared. The oldest skips school; the fourteen-year-old is a "perfect" student, immerses herself in many school activities, but is depressed; the twelve-year-old is angry and gets into fights in the neighborhood; the eight-year-old cries a lot; and the youngest will be repeating

kindergarten because of his "immaturity." Neither parent likes the court-ordered parenting plan. Maria wants the kids to have supervised visitation with their dad since he is emotionally abusive to her. Sean wants custody of the kids since they are struggling academically and emotionally. Like most children of divorce, the kids wish their parents had never gotten divorced; they routinely sabotage potentially new relationships for both parents. In their view, their parents argue more now than when they were married.

Research over the last fifteen years[1] suggests that children have the hardest time adjusting to a divorce when the parents remain in a high level of conflict, and keep the children in the middle of the conflict. The hardest job for parents is to recognize when their behavior adds to the level of conflict, and when this increases the tension and stress for their children.

The first step in improving things for your children is to recognize how your behavior contributes to the conflicts with your ex. It is easy to recognize obvious behavior that contributes to conflict: frequent court battles, arguing in front of your children (especially at the children's activities), harsh words at the drop-off and pick-up of your children, negative tone of voice, arguing over the phone within earshot of your child. Even if you are not aware of how such conflict *affects* your children, it is important to recognize that you are engaging in such behaviors.

Unfortunately, you may not be able to recognize more subtle forms of conflict and the impact it has upon your children. Your attitude about your child's relationship with the other parent will certainly affect how your child adjusts to your divorce. Positive feelings help, while anger and other negative feelings will increase your child's stress and possibly lead to loyalty conflicts. This chapter addresses both the subtle and obvious behaviors that raise the level of conflict, disrupt your children's relationships, and increase levels of distress.

Understand Your Level of Conflict

While research is unable to precisely measure the extent to which parents engage in different levels of conflict, California psychologist and best-selling author Constance Ahrons[2] has identified four primary styles in which parents interact. One such style, referred to by Ahrons as "Parenting Pals" reflects *relatively low conflict*, in that the parents generally cooperate with each other, share their children and follow their parenting plan, participate together in their children's activities, and are truly able to set aside their differences for their children.

A rather sizeable number of families experience a *moderate degree of conflict*. Ahrons referred to these two groups as either "Cooperative Colleagues," in which they had somewhat less conflict, or "Angry Associates," in which their anger was worse and conflicts were more intense. Such parents might get fairly tense with one another and keep their distance at their children's activities, yet they are able to maintain a fairly businesslike approach to dealing with the tasks of parenting. They inform each other of important details about the children and are polite to one another in public. They are generally able to make agreements for their children's extracurricular activities, medical needs, vacations and holidays. Parents in this group are able to talk to each other reasonably well about their children's needs, and set aside their differences most of the time in order to meet these needs. Within this group, however, there may be a general level of tension and some difficulty reaching agreements. While things might go smoothly for several months, it's easy for families in this group to have major arguments, sometimes over the simplest of things. These parents may be likely to say negative things about each other to the child. One or both parents might become stubborn, making it easy to fall into a pattern of arguing — similar to that exhibited during the marriage. It is very common for families to be at this stage of conflict for the first year or two after separation, and then move to a more peaceful relationship after several years. It is this level of conflict that is sometimes hard to identify because things appear easy much of the time. However, when problems do surface, it is easy for arguments to intensify. Jim and Kathy, described in the Introduction, fall into this category.

A third group of divorced families — research suggests perhaps fifteen-to-twenty percent — may exhibit a *very high level of conflict*. Ahrons referred to them as "Fiery Foes." From the children's perspective, this level of conflict is the worst. Arguments sometimes erupt into violence, police get called to settle visitation disputes, and enforcement of court orders is difficult. These parents may go back to court several times in a year, attempting to reach an agreement on their differences. Children may not be able to participate in extracurricular activities because Dad will want the little league games in his neighborhood while Mom wants them in hers. Even if their child is able to sign up for little league, they can't agree on who's responsible for purchasing the equipment, and they blame each other when the baseball glove is left at the other parent's house. Arguments might even erupt at ball games. Many of these children are hyper-vigilant, constantly worrying about whether or not their parents will create a scene in public.

If you are like other divorcing parents in such high-conflict families, you will probably believe that the other parent *causes* about seventy-five to eighty percent of the conflict. However, I have found that either parent — by her or his own actions — can actually *prevent* about seventy-five to eighty percent of the conflict. It is my belief that the best way to *win* an argument is to not *participate* in the argument!

Conflict-Producing Behavior

Conflicts can occur in so many areas, including attitudes, schedules, extra-curricular activities, communication, new partners, schooling, parenting philosophy, clothing and your child's "things." Here are a few examples of parent-conflict behaviors, how they affect your children, and what you can do about them.

❖   ❖   ❖   ❖   ❖

Eight-year-old Jeremy is supposed to see his dad every other weekend from Friday at 6:00 p.m. until returning to his mother on Sunday at 6:00 p.m. Jeremy's mom places Jeremy in a difficult position about once a month when she arranges a family camping trip on Dad's weekend. Jeremy is aware that his mom and her relatives are going camping and she typically says to him, "If you would rather go with us than see your dad, why don't you let him know." At other times, she might say, "It's probably pretty boring at your dad's since you don't have any friends over there." She may slip in other negative statements about Dad, as well. By putting Jeremy in the middle — fun with her family or being with his dad — she is hoping that Jeremy will call his father and beg to be allowed to go camping, putting Dad in a difficult spot. If Dad says "No," Jeremy will resent it, and if he says, "Yes, it's okay to go camping," he loses time with Jeremy, especially if Mom doesn't willingly trade weekends. Neither of these parents perceive themselves as "angry associates," but their behaviors consistently appear that way.

With that in mind, you should only plan special activities, such as a favorite camping trip, during your time with your child. Look at your schedule first, and only schedule these events when your child is with you. It's important to pay attention to your child's schedule, arrange activities that include the children when the children are with you, and schedule activities without the children when they are going to be with the other parent. This will send a message of support to your child — and the other parent — regarding the value that you place on your child's time with the other parent.

There will be times, of course, when the timing of an event is beyond your control, and you have no choice but to arrange activities with your child during the time she is scheduled to be with the other parent. Perhaps a relative is visiting from far away. Or a special sports event or concert may come up (one that you — and not your ex — typically share with your child). When that happens, request the other parent's permission to invite the child to the event *before* you talk with your child about it, and volunteer in *advance* to trade time, if necessary. After the other parent has okayed the request, then invite your child. If you and the other parent can't agree on the request, don't tell your child about it. Following these steps can help reduce tension by *keeping your child out of the middle.*

❖   ❖   ❖   ❖   ❖

Suzy has been nervous and scared ever since her parents separated. She goes to preschool while both of her parents work. Dad picks her up every Monday and Tuesday, Mom every Wednesday and Thursday, and she alternates weekends with each parent. Both parents are nurturing and careful not to say anything bad about the other parent. Additionally, each parent allows Suzy the opportunity to speak daily with the other parent in order to ease her transition. The daily routine, however, is extremely different at each house. Mom is relatively structured, with dinner made within a half-hour of when she gets home, followed by play time, and then a routine for bath and bed. Suzy sleeps in her own bed at Mom's house. She is never late for preschool, always arriving at 7:30 in the morning, and she is picked up at 5:00 p.m.

On the other hand, because Dad's work life is fairly unstructured, his routine with Suzy is hard to follow. On some days, he drops her off as early as 6:30 a.m. and doesn't pick her up until 6:00 p.m., when she is the last child there. On other days, he doesn't take her to school until 9:30 or 10:00 in the morning, and he might pick her up as early as 3:00 p.m. Dinnertime and bedtime are random and inconsistent, depending on Dad's needs at the end of the day.

Given her young age, it is difficult for Suzy to keep track of who is picking her up. Neither Mom nor Dad talk with her about the schedule, which adds to Suzy's confusion. Suzy sometimes misses out on activities at school and with friends because her parents do not communicate with each other. The differences in routine and the lack of communication between the parents create tension and insecurity for Suzy, making her adjustment to the divorce quite difficult. While Mom and Dad think they are doing the right thing by avoiding conflict and saying only positive things about each other, they don't realize that their lack of communication creates instability and insecurity for Suzy.

In spite of the fact that these parents probably perceive themselves as "cooperative colleagues," their lack of communication makes it difficult for Suzy.

The solution for Suzy would be for her parents to talk with one another on a regular basis and make their routines — at least those affecting Suzy — more consistent. It would be particularly helpful in reducing Suzy's anxiety if Dad could make his routines more structured. Because a three-year-old child does not have a mature sense of dates and time, her own calendar (with color-coding or graphics to make it "readable" for her) would help her know who is picking her up at the end of each day. (Developmental issues will be addressed in more detail in chapter 4.) It would also be wise for the school to be aware of the schedule and the approximate time Suzy will be picked up each day, allowing her teacher to comfort and support Suzy if she shows signs of anxiety or insecurity. Each parent should establish a strong, *independent* relationship with the school staff, so each of them can keep track of Suzy's functioning at school and be aware of school activities so Suzy doesn't lose out.

❖   ❖   ❖   ❖   ❖

Dana, age 7, and Robbie, age 9, alternate weeks between their parents. Mom and Dad don't talk to each other, so all communication goes through the children. When the time and place of Dana's soccer game gets changed, Dana has to call her dad and tell him about it. When Robbie has a big homework assignment due the following week, he has to call Mom and let her know. Mom and Dad do not actively argue in front of the children; in fact, they rarely see each other. Their style of parenting is considered "Disengaged," as they generally avoid contact with one another as much as possible. Unfortunately, both of these parents become angry when activities fail, largely because all of their communication goes through the children. For example, if Dana misses her soccer game, Dad blames her for being irresponsible and not getting the time right. When Robbie does not complete his school assignment on time, Mom grounds him for the week that he is in her care. The children get blamed and punished for problems that occur because *they* are being asked to do the *parent's* job of communicating. The children become frustrated and have a difficult time with their own anger and insecurity. They are tired of being blamed when things go wrong. When they express their frustration to their parents, the parents accuse each other of creating the problem, never taking responsibility for anything.

The solution for Dana and Robbie would be for Mom and Dad to share schedules and communicate changes. They may need professional help learning new styles of communication. Ultimately, if they cannot learn to manage the children's schedules, they may need to adjust the parenting plan so that one or the other has primary parenting responsibility (custody). Parents need to be the adults, take the responsibility to share communication, and not blame their children. When parents share parenting in a significant manner, it is critical that the parents communicate with each other about the details and not rely on the children to pass messages back and forth.

❖   ❖   ❖   ❖   ❖

Jessica, 11, spends alternate weeks with each parent. She feels the tension between her parents, who argue with each other whenever they are together. As difficult as this is, however, she has a harder time dealing with the fact that all communication goes through her, unless it is in writing. When her mother writes her father a letter about something, he throws the letter at Jessica and says to her, "This is why I can't deal with your mother." He then has Jessica read the letter. Dad always tells Jessica how uncooperative Mom is. Added to this, Mom will always remind Jessica whenever the child support check is late, saying such things to her as, "If I don't get your dad's check soon, we might have to move because I can't pay the rent." Whenever Jessica tells her mom of the enjoyable things that she does at Dad's, Mom always says, "Of course he can take you there, honey, because he never pays me what he's supposed to." Jessica can't have fun or enjoy her relationship with either parent.

Jessica's parents are "Fiery Foes," as they argue all of the time, generally despise each other, and never communicate in a positive way. If Jessica's mom and dad don't change their style of interacting and stop dumping their anger onto Jessica, she most likely will grow up resenting both of her parents and wondering what's likely to go wrong whenever she's enjoying herself. Clearly, their actions are detrimental to her overall emotional health.

❖   ❖   ❖   ❖   ❖

In all these ways and more, your behavior has the potential of putting tremendous pressure on your children. You don't want to do this, yet it's hard to recognize when your behavior is damaging to your child. Some behaviors are particularly likely to add to the intensity of conflict your children feel, and to make it more difficult for your children to accept and adjust to your divorce and life in general:

- Derogatory statements about the other parent
- Telling children about child support problems
- Showing children the letters that your ex-spouse has written or showing the children court papers
- Failing to communicate and forcing communication to be through the children
- Talking about courts and the judge
- Asking children to make decisions about where they want to live
- Tempting children with fun activities when they're supposed to be with the other parent.

When children are subjected to *any* of these behaviors, it is like a bomb going off in the middle of a war — and we all know that prisoners of war carry wounds with them long after the fighting has stopped.

The Wounds of Fighting

When fighting continues after the divorce, children become disillusioned and disgusted. When parents divorce, children hope the fighting will go away so that they can have some peace in their lives. Research suggests that children have the hardest time adjusting to a divorce when parents are in medium or high conflict before a divorce and remain in high conflict after the divorce. Many times I have heard children say that they wouldn't mind the divorce so much if their parents would finally learn to get along better. After the divorce, all children really want is for their parents to act grown up, take good care of them, leave them in peace, and let them love the other parent. Instead, when conflicts worsen, children are left with many wounds.

These wounds can include feelings of disillusionment, fear, insecurity, vulnerability, and prolonged frustration, among others. Children develop loyalty conflicts and become afraid to love both parents or express their love for one parent in front of the other parent. Many of these children become aligned with only one parent in an attempt to feel less anxious and insecure. This is a factor in alienated children, described in more detail in chapter 10. Children frequently feel that they have failed or done something wrong when the conflicts occur, and feel even more insecure when they can't prevent the arguments.

At its worst, children experiencing intense conflict have to take sides because they can't manage the internal tension and anxiety they feel. For these children, there is a risk of serious psychological regression where they will see one parent as mostly bad and the other parent as mostly good. This psychological "splitting," as it is called, is damaging to children because it reinforces a style in which they view the world in a "black-and-white" or "all-or-nothing" way, rather than a more balanced view of both good *and* bad in people and situations. Children in this situation often create distortions in their thinking, for example, as they state unequivocally that a parent has harmed them, in spite of the absence of any abuse. Psychological splitting and cognitive distortions, in my experience, are the most destructive emotional symptoms that children might experience as a result of their parents' conflict largely because of the confusion and anxiety it creates.

Children are likely to express their emotional wounds with such behavior patterns as regression, aggression, withdrawal, or depression. They show signs of increased insecurity in the transition between homes and may be reluctant to express affection. They may feel embarrassed, daydream a lot, worry excessively, and have trouble in school. They are likely to feel responsible for their parent's conflicts, and be more edgy emotionally. They might become clingy with one or both of you. In young children, signs of regression can include bedwetting and temper tantrums. School-age children often have difficulty with schoolwork, peers, and/or behavior problems in the classroom or neighborhood. Other school-age children might withdraw from friends and activities. By the time children reach adolescence, they are at risk of expressing their wounds with rebelliousness, substance abuse, inappropriate sexual activity, and/or other serious or self-destructive behaviors.

While it is common for parents to blame each other when these symptoms erupt, it is important to recognize that y*ou likely play a role* in these difficulties. You need to recognize that both your obvious — and not-so-obvious — behaviors are likely to be pressuring your children and causing them to feel a particular way. The very act of blaming the other parent can cause your children to feel bad and act out.

Here are a few steps you can take toward reducing unnecessary conflict:

- Watch your children for signs of the emotional wounds described above

- Recognize and take responsibility for your own role in any conflict with your ex

- Improve your communication with the other parent and with your children

- Reduce your own role in the conflict by not participating

- Ease your children's transition between homes so that they can be free of the tension that results from parental conflict at contact times.

Talking with Your Children in a Healthy Way

Research suggests that parents often tell their children very little about the separation and divorce at the time of the separation. This increases children's anxiety and insecurity, as they don't understand what is happening in their family. From the time you first separate, you need to begin talking to your children in a healthy way. Your children are likely to have many questions about your divorce, and they may need to ask questions many different times as they grow. Their ability to understand the divorce is always dependent on age and cognitive abilities, as well as how emotionally ready they are to hear what you are telling them. There are both healthy and destructive ways to talk to your children, and it is your responsibility to speak about the divorce in the healthiest way possible.

Tell your children about the divorce as soon as you have made a decision to separate. You must reassure your children that they will be loved, that it is not their fault, and that both parents will continue to be involved in their lives. Pay attention to your child's initial insecurity and answer questions about why the divorce is taking place, what he can expect about changes in his life, etc. Do this without blaming the other parent. Build your own adult support network — including therapy if you need it — to make sure you are emotionally strong enough so that your child is not taking care of your feelings.

Many parents assume that they will only need to talk about the divorce once. As you adjust to your divorce, you might make the assumption that your child is doing the same and that questions will not resurface. However, if your child is three or four when you divorce, she may not ask the important questions that will certainly come to the surface later. Because she didn't think of them when she was little, as she grows she may have new questions regarding your divorce. It is important to acknowledge periodically to your child that the divorce has been difficult. Wonder aloud if she has any new questions or thoughts that she wants to talk about.

Stop and Think

It's critical for you to stop and think before you say things that might be damaging to your children. You know it is important to avoid loud arguments in front of your children, but you need to remember to avoid put-downs, derogatory statements, or other comments that cause problems as well. Be mindful of your tone of voice. Avoid using the divorce as an excuse for your child's behavior problems. Your words can be damaging to your child, especially when she is feeling caught in the middle of your conflict.

Ultimately, you need to talk to your children about responsibility. Encourage your child to talk about things that are frustrating to him, and offer to help him avoid getting caught in the middle of your conflicts with the other parent. Avoid blaming the other parent when problems erupt. Encourage each other — and your kids — to understand each person's individual role in the problems. Avoid placing blame, making negative statements about the other parent, and including your children in your conflicts. By doing so, your children can avoid the battle wounds. (See chapter 5 for specific examples about how to answer your child's questions and comments.)

Easing Your Child's Transition Between Homes

Research supports the idea that children can function relatively well in two households after a divorce.[3] However, parents must do several things to help their child handle a regular and consistent transition between two homes. The most important thing that you can offer your child is an attitude of sharing and cooperation, and an acceptance that the child needs a healthy relationship with both parents. If children experience an attitude of sharing and cooperation, they can relax as they move back and forth between homes on a schedule that flows with the routines of the family.

On the other hand, if children are worried about your response to their relationship with the other parent, they will feel anxiety and tension, which will likely cause unhealthy symptoms during their transition. These symptoms might include clinging, withdrawal, agitation, and aggression. Instead of criticizing, bring a healthy attitude to your child's transition between homes. Do this whether you have primary custody (your child is going to the other parent for a weekend visit), share joint physical custody (your child is going to the other parent for the week), or live far apart (your child is going to see the other parent for six weeks in the summer). The most important gift you can give your child is a healthy attitude about the time that he will spend with his other parent.

You can do other things to ease the tension at your child's transitions. If you and your ex-spouse are at the same location at the transfer time, be polite, and avoid talking about anything that will stir up conflict. In other words, act friendly or cooperatively, without harsh interactions. Plan the exchanges with your usual level of conflict in mind. If you can be together with little conflict, it is usually best for you to pick up your child to bring her to your house. This allows your daughter to make sure that she has all of her belongings as she takes them from one parent's home to the next. You can then use the drive home as a way of beginning the transition from the other home to yours. For most children when their parents are in low conflict, this is the easiest way make the transition.

On the other hand, if there is frequent conflict when you are with one another, it is probably better if the other parent drops the child at your home. This way, the originating parent and the child can gather the child's things and take them to your house, saying their good-byes to each other before they arrive. With this approach, you don't have to interact with your ex-spouse and conflict can be avoided. If there is typically a moderate level of conflict between the two of you, this reduces the burdens on your children.

The third option, especially if you and your ex-spouse engage in significant conflict, is to avoid interaction altogether when that's possible. School or daycare can be used as the site for dropping off and picking up the children. The school or daycare thus becomes a buffer in the transition between homes. For families where there is a very high degree of conflict, or when parents have a difficult time being in the same place together, this is the best arrangement. If the parents share joint physical custody, and the children spend alternate weeks at each parent's home, Friday or Monday may be the best day of transfer. Arranging it in relation to the drop off and pick up from school is the easiest way to avoid problems in transition.

Determining *in advance* how to manage your children's belongings and activities will also ease the transition. Don't be angry with your child when she leaves something at the other parent's house. Remember, *you* got divorced, *she* didn't. Just go and get it for her. As I will outline in chapter 6, it is important for children to have clothing at both homes so that they do not have to transport clothes back and forth. During the school year, it is likely that your children will need to transport and keep track of school projects and other work. Throughout the year, recreational and extracurricular items will need to be moved between homes. Especially for children younger than 14, it is *your responsibility, not your child's,* to make sure that the needed items are transferred. If your child spends time worrying about his things or if he gets blamed when something isn't where you think it belongs, he will feel angry or insecure, and may develop symptoms like those described above. There are plenty of opportunities to teach your children individual responsibility that have nothing to do with their parents' choice to live in two homes.

Small items are easy to place in a backpack. When your child goes to school in the morning, she will have what she needs. When she goes to the other parent's home in the evening, no transfer of items is required. For large items, remember, your child doesn't want to take a suitcase to school! It is awkward and embarrassing. Until your child can drive, it is your responsibility to develop a plan for transferring bigger items. Make every effort to avoid conflict, as you and your ex share equal responsibility for the transfers. Since both of you have a vested interest in your child's success at school, both of you must cooperate in the transfer of homework and school projects from one house to the other. Schools can sometimes assist parents by providing two sets of books, so that books don't have to be moved between homes. (Chapter 6 provides more detail for solutions in transferring your child's items between homes.)

Ultimately, you need to have a healthy attitude in order to ease the transition and move your child's belongings between your two homes. Here are some additional helpful steps:

- Call your child on the night before the transition
- Talk about the necessary items for transfer
- Reassure him of the drop off and pick up time and place
- Discuss the activities you have planned for the next few days

Once your child is at your home, give him time to settle and reconnect with you and your environment. Your child is likely to be a bit confused during transition time. Some children call their mom "Dad," or vice-versa. This is normal. Other children may forget the rules or routines. Do not criticize or punish your child for such normal activities. If you maintain a relaxed attitude about the transition, your child is more likely to be relaxed as well. This is especially important when there is some discrepancy in the rules and routines in each home. If you have other siblings in your home, the reconnection may be made easier through them — especially if you make a special effort to enlist their cooperation.

Most importantly, don't quiz your children about what takes place in the other parent's home. Your children love both of you, and feel a strong loyalty to each of you. When you question them about what happens in the other parent's home, they are likely to feel anxious and defensive and will avoid sharing information. Encourage your children to share what they want to share, but avoid asking questions that raise stress levels and cause anxiety.

Stop and think about all aspects of your post-divorce behavior and its impact on your children. By putting your child's needs first, you can avoid conflicts that hurt your child, and you can support your child's healthy relationship with the other parent. If each parent takes the time and the responsibility to reduce conflict, you can encourage your children to develop a healthy adjustment to your divorce, and avoid the insecurities and traumas that some children of divorce experience.

Things to Remember

Conflicts between parents are likely to cause:
- tension, anxiety, and regression
- feelings of confusion and embarrassment

- feelings of responsibility and self-blame in your kids
- withdrawal or clinging behavior at transitions
- long-term emotional and behavioral wounds
- feelings of disillusionment, fear, insecurity, or vulnerability
- psychological or social withdrawal and avoidance of friends or extra-curricular activities
- temper tantrums, school problems, or self-destructive behaviors

You can ease your child's transitions by:
- promoting and supporting an atmosphere of cooperation and sharing with the other parent
- periodically talking with your child about the schedule to see if it needs improvements
- keeping the transfer of the children free of conflict
- using your child's school or daycare as a buffer zone if you can't avoid conflict
- working with the other parent to maintain responsibility for transporting your children's belongings
- using phone calls to begin the transition process
- giving your children time to reconnect

From Conflict to Cooperation
- Conflicts that hurt your children can be both subtle and obvious.
- Stop blaming each other and avoid derogatory comments.
- Change your own behavior to help reduce the conflicts.
- Talk with your children in a healthy way.
- Communicate with each other and stop using your children as messengers.
- Take responsibility for your own behavior.

Notes

[1] See e.g., Kelly, J.B. & Emery, R.E. Children's Adjustment Following Divorce: Risk and Resilience Perspectives. *Family Relations*, Vol. 52, No. 4, pgs. 352-362, 2003; Kelly, J.B. Children's Adjustment in Conflicted Marriage and Divorce: A Decade Review of Research. *Journal of the American*

Academy of Child & Adolescent Psychiatry, Vol. 39, No. 8, pgs. 963-973, 2000; Hetherington, M. & Kelly, J. *For Better or Worse: Divorce Reconsidered.* New York: Norton, 2003.

2 Ahrons, C., *We're Still Family: What Grown Children Have to Say about Their Parent's Divorce.* New York: Harper Paperbacks, 2005.

3 Bauserman, R. Child Adjustment in Joint-custody Versus Sole-custody Arrangements: A Meta-analytic Review. *Journal of Family Psychology*, Vol 16, No. 1, pgs. 91–102, 2002.

CHAPTER 2

It's Time for a Truce

Parenting Plans Promote Peace

"If two people always agree, one is superfluous, if they always disagree, both are superfluous."
—Anonymous

AS WE DISCUSSED in chapter 1, it is very difficult for children when parents continue to argue. This is especially true if your children feel caught in the middle of your dispute, either because they are being used as messengers or spies, or just because they are overhearing you talk with others about your divorce. Because conflict can be so damaging to your child, the greatest gift that you can give your child is to find a more peaceful way of dealing with your conflicts. This means learning to resolve your differences, or at least debate the issues out of your child's earshot.

There are many things that you can do to help yourself handle your feelings constructively. There are also many strategies that you can use to reduce the opportunities for conflict. In this chapter, we'll discuss a few:

- Understand your level of conflict
- Determine whether you can cooperatively parent or will need to parallel parent
- Develop a thorough parenting plan
- Learn how to compromise and call for a truce

This chapter is designed to address these opportunities.

Cooperative Parenting or Parallel Parenting?

Research on families of divorce suggests that there are primarily three styles of parenting for families after a divorce: *cooperative, conflicted,* or *disengaged. Cooperative* parenting is the style used by families in which conflict is low and parents can effectively communicate about their child. If you determine that your level of conflict is low, you and the other parent will probably be able to talk about your child's needs in a healthy way. You will probably agree on most parenting values, be relatively consistent in your parenting styles, and have few arguments about your child's life. You will rarely put your child in the middle, and you will solve differences peacefully. Research shows that children of divorce adjust best when parents can be cooperative in their parenting. If you fall in this category, you should feel good about yourselves and know that you are helping your child immensely. There are many good books on cooperative parenting designed to help parents do a more effective job. A list of several such books will be found in Appendix A.

As mentioned in the Introduction, however, this book focuses on those parents who are in *conflict* and argue a lot or need to disengage in their parenting. Even if you can sometimes parent cooperatively, you may find it to be difficult to do so and find yourself in conflict too much of the time. Conflicted parenting after divorce is quite difficult for children, especially when your child is in the middle of your conflicts. Your children will adjust to your divorce easier if you can avoid conflicted parenting. There are many factors that contribute to conflicted parenting. The psychological issues that lead to conflicted parenting are many, and may include:

- continuation of hostility that began during the marriage
- differing perceptions of pre-separation child-rearing roles
- differing perceptions of post-separation child-rearing roles
- differing perceptions of how to parent
- concern about the adequacy of the other parent's parenting ability
- an unwillingness on the part of one or both parents to accept the end of the relationship
- jealousy about a new partner in the other parent's life
- contested child custody issues
- personality traits in one or both parents that stimulate conflict.

Whatever the specific source, a parent's inability to separate their parental roles from prior conflict in the marriage is a significant contribution to the conflict after the divorce. As described in chapter 1, this conflict is perhaps the most important variable in determining how your child will adjust to your divorce. It is important to do whatever it takes to change your level of conflict.

The first step in this process is to learn to *disengage* from the other parent. Disengagement is one of the possible styles of parenting after divorce. If you disengage, it's like you have developed a "demilitarized zone" around your children and have little or no contact with the other parent. When you disengage, you will not respond to your ex's efforts to push your buttons. Essentially, you will avoid contact with the other parent so that conflict cannot develop. Disengagement is a critical first step if you want to reduce the conflict and before you can move on to the next style of parenting.

The second step in this process is what I call *parallel parenting*. In this style of parenting, both of you will each learn to parent your child effectively, doing the best job each of you can do during the time you are with your child. You will continue to disengage from the other parent so that conflicts are avoided. If you determine that you cannot cooperatively parent because your level of conflict is moderate or high, disengagement and parallel parenting is the necessary style of parenting.

Parallel parenting gets its name from a similar concept in children's play. Research psychologists have observed that young children who play together, but do not have the skills to interact, engage in a process of parallel play. If they are in a sandbox together or taking turns going down a slide, they play *next* to one another, not *with* one another. Each child is doing her own thing with the toys, and generally ignoring the other. When they get older, they will learn to interact cooperatively and play *together*.

Similarly, parallel parenting is a process of parenting next to one another because you are unable to parent together. Before you can learn to co-parent, you will each learn to parent on your own. The first step of parallel parenting is disengagement. This means that you will not communicate about minor things regarding your child. You will not bicker over things that have always led to conflicts in the past. You will give the other parent important information about your child, but you will not get into debates about the parenting plan or about each other's parenting style.

"Important information" means the health, welfare, and interests of your child. If your child is sick, you will inform the other parent of this fact, with details on what medication is needed, what has already been administered, and when the next dose is to be given. If your child has a school field trip, you will inform the other parent of the details, and use your parenting plan to decide who might go with the child on the field trip. Each of you should develop independent relationships with your child's teachers, doctors, coaches, and friends so that you don't have to rely on the other parent to receive important information. Each of you should take turns taking your child to the doctor and dentist. If you are the parent who receives your child's report card, copy it and send it to the other parent. Do this with medical and extra-curricular activity information, such as your child's little league schedule. Do not complain to the other parent when she is ten minutes late for an exchange of your child, and don't argue over whose turn it is to get your child's next haircut. Have parameters in your parenting plan for some of these things and ignore the rest.

When parents are trying to disengage, but communication is necessary, it is often best for all non-emergency communication to be done by mail, fax or e-mail. Only use faxes if both of you have sufficient privacy where you will receive the fax. By putting your communication in writing, you will have time to gather your thoughts and make sure that the tone is not argumentative. This also lets the receiving parent take some time and gather his thoughts so that he is not impulsive or angry in his response. Sarcasm is never helpful when trying to disengage from conflicts. Don't share your e-mails and faxes with your children; they are simply meant to share important information between the parents. Try to limit non-emergency communication to twice a month, except for sharing information that is time-sensitive (like faxing a notice from school to the other parent on the day you receive it). Obviously, emergency information about illnesses and injuries, unforeseen delays in visitation (as a result of traffic conditions, for example), or immediate school concerns should be shared by phone as soon as possible. Especially if you must be late for an exchange due to traffic conditions, use a mobile phone to expedite this communication. However, by reducing verbal communication for all but non-emergency communication, and by putting necessary communications in writing, you will go a long way toward disengaging from conflict.

If you have very young children, you know it is important to share all aspects of your child's functions with the care provider when you drop her off. In the same way, it is critical for parents to share detailed information with each other upon the exchange of the child. A useful tool is a "parent communication notebook." In this notebook you will write down the highlights of your child's emotions and behaviors during the time she's with you. Fill out the notebook in great detail and pass it along to the other parent at the time of transition. Things to include in this notebook are your observations of your child's health, feeding and sleeping patterns, your child's developing language, observations about your child's mood, what upsets your child and what soothes your child, your daily routine, and any other detailed information about your child's functions and needs. This notebook should stay with your child so both parents can use it as a forum for preserving thoughts about your child and her needs.

Another key to parallel parenting is avoiding telling the other parent how to parent, and ignoring (rather than arguing back) when the other parent tries to tell you how to parent. Recognize that it is better to encourage different parenting styles rather than get into conflict over those styles. Obviously, some things are very important, such as consistent discipline philosophies and techniques, adequate supervision, giving your child necessary medication, and ensuring that your child gets to school on time with homework completed. If you have concerns about these very important issues, you will need a forum for working out your differences. I will discuss several ideas in chapter 9.

However, there are many things that parents argue about that aren't so important. Some of this is related to different parenting philosophies and some of it is related to the difficulty of sharing your child. Accept that there is more than one "right way" to parent. Learn to be less rigid and more accepting of your child's other parent. Rather than trying to change how the other parent does his job of parenting, do your best job of parenting during the time your child is with you, without criticizing the other parent. Children are capable of being parented with different styles of parenting, and many children of divorce adjust quite well to two very different homes. Remember, just as you will want to avoid criticizing the other parent, you will not want to deal with criticism of your parenting techniques. There will be more elaboration on this topic in chapter 7.

The Concept of a Parenting Plan
To really support your child and develop a truce, abide by your marital settlement agreement, the court orders, and your parenting plan. Focus on your child, not the conflicts with your ex-spouse.

In the process of getting a divorce, a marital settlement agreement is developed which outlines the legal terms and conditions of your divorce. In most states, this will include information about your financial settlement, arrangements for spousal and child support, distribution of property, and custody of your children. While the financial and property distribution is often described in exact detail (sometimes including who gets what furniture or Aunt Mary's china), the custody arrangements and parenting plan is often inadequate. Divorcing couples who are able to cooperate easily may only need a few paragraphs to describe a parenting plan, but many families find that the standard language of a custody order is so vague that they disagree about almost everything. A detailed parenting plan can help you with this.

Parenting plans are not "one size fits all." There are no specific rules about what is needed in a parenting plan. Because conflict can be so high for many families, there is consideration in some states to mandate that a divorce cannot be finalized until a parenting plan is in place. The amount of detail in your parenting plan will depend on the level of conflict you have with your ex-spouse. In this section, I will detail what you might want to include in a parenting plan if you and the other parent are generally in a higher level of conflict. You may not need all of this detail, but you might find that more detail is needed than you think so that there is less room for conflict in the future. If you create a careful and well-thought-out parenting plan, you can save considerable aggravation later. Of course, once you have a parenting plan, it is critical that you abide by it. If you have a parenting plan and then continue to argue about its details or its meaning, your children will have a difficult time. However, if you take the time and energy to develop a careful parenting plan and then use your parenting plan as your guide to caring for your children, you will be teaching your child the benefit of problem solving and conflict resolution.

Take a look at the sample parenting plan (Appendix B). The elements of a parenting plan usually include the following:

• A *schedule that is clear and well defined*. It cannot be adjusted by either parent without mutual agreement, usually in writing. It usually specifies how holidays and vacations will be arranged, and defines the nature of the exchange. It should also include the procedures by which a parent can request a one-time change in the schedule. It's important to clarify who makes the ultimate decision when there's a disagreement. You might even alternate who makes these decisions; for example, Mom in even-numbered years and Dad in odd-numbered years. This is quite helpful for school vacation periods and travel plans.

• A clause describing *how parents will decide who will be responsible* for the children when a parent is unavailable during his or her custodial time. Some parents will have a "right of first refusal," and other parents will get baby-sitters or leave the children with relatives when they cannot be available to care for their children. Both are acceptable for your children and hopefully will not be a source of conflict for the two of you.

- A clause describing *who will provide transportation* of the children between the parent's homes. Usually, it's best for children if the receiving parent picks up the children, either at a neutral site or at the other parent's home.

- A clause about *ultimate decision-making for children*. Typically, the parent who has physical custody makes the day-to-day decisions for the child. The parenting plan defines this, and defines how major decisions will get made.

- A *forum for managing disputes* about major decisions, especially as more parents have joint legal custody. This may include decisions about school, medical, and extra-curricular activities. A parenting plan will frequently have a clause about methods for resolving impasses. Ideas such as mediation, arbitration, use of a special master or parenting coordinator, and other forms of dispute resolution will be discussed in chapter 9.

- A provision for *modification and review as special circumstances arise* or developmental needs change, especially when parents divorce with young children or were never married.

- A clause outlining *financial responsibilities* and who will pay for things related to the day-to-day parenting of children. The parenting plan will usually describe a mechanism for verifying the extra expenses that aren't covered by child support or reimbursed by health insurance.

- A clause associated with the *responsibilities of parenting* that may include who will stay home from work when children are sick, who will go on school field trips, who will take the children to non-emergency medical and dental appointments, who will help with homework, and who will participate with the children in extra-curricular activities.

- Provisions for parents to *share necessary information* with each other (i.e., school, medical care, and activities).

- A clause associated with your child's *religious education* and who is responsible for maintaining it.

- Specific information for *renegotiating the parenting plan* and re-assessing the children's needs in case of a future move by either parent.

Choose parts of this parenting plan that will meet your needs, making sure all areas of potential conflict are covered.

Outline of the Elements of a Parenting Plan*

General Philosophy
Description of specific legal custody as determined by the court. Statement of the desire of the parents to be cooperative and mutually responsible for the care of the child(ren). Declaration to place the needs of the child(ren) first. Descriptions of how major decisions are to be made, how parents' new relationships affect the plan, and how personal possessions of the child(ren) will be taken care of. "Sets the stage" for an agreement based on mutual respect, responsibility, and consideration for the child(ren) and both parents.

Parenting Schedule
Specific guidelines with regard to where the child will be when, and which parent is responsible at each time. Who will pick up and drop off the child, at what time, and where the pick-up or drop off will occur. Description of procedures for weekend and overnight visits, both during the school year and non-school year. Detailed schedules and plans for holidays, vacations, and birthdays.

Parental Contributions
How much each parent will contribute toward food and shelter, insurance, medical and dental care, clothing, education, extra-curricular activities, and recreation. Procedures for parent consultation regarding non-emergency, non-covered medical costs.

Communication and Conflict Resolution
How communication and conflict resolution should take place. Procedures for a "communication book" for recording messages. Statement of agreement to make major decisions jointly (i.e., regarding education, health care, childcare, religious training), rather than unilaterally. Steps for achieving resolution when agreement cannot be reached, or if modification is desired.

Miscellaneous
Ties up "loose ends." Provides instructions regarding everyday situations: who will care for the child during illness; what are the responsibilities when out-of-town travel is planned; how frequently and in what manner will telephone access (or other means of communication) occur; details about transportation to various activities; miscellaneous day-to-day decisions, such as bedtime, hygiene, curfew, chores; how and when will parents keep each other informed of emergencies; responsibilities regarding sharing of information; and possible relocation of a parent.

Review of Agreement
Arrangements (e.g., time and place) for review of the parenting plan.

---

* (For a sample detailed parenting plan, see Appendix B.)

Avoiding Conflict When the Other Parent Wants to Fight

It can be very difficult to have good boundaries with the other parent and know when to either ignore the other parent or hold firm when discussing a particular issue. The first principle in this process is to take some time and stop and think about the issue and how important it really is. Is your hesitation about your child, or is it about your typical conflict pattern? Think about whether your ex-spouse is being reasonable in her request, and whether or not you might actually ask a similar favor of her. As you think about the issues at hand, ask yourself if it seems reasonable, and likely that you might make a similar request in the future. If so, you would certainly want to go along with the request.

This style of communication requires two significant components. First, if you are requesting a favor of the other parent, it must come in the form of a request and not as a demand. For example, many parents do not have a beginning and ending time of holidays on their parenting plan. Suppose you normally do not have your children overnight when they are with you on Sunday, but this year you have the Fourth of July, which is on Sunday. You want to keep the children overnight, and you recognize that neither of you has to work the next day. Rather than saying to your ex-spouse, "I'm keeping the kids until 10:00 tomorrow morning," it's much less antagonizing if you say, "Is there any problem with my keeping the kids until 10:00 tomorrow morning? Neither of us are going to work and I want to take them to the fireworks display tonight." Thus, the first step in the communication process is to make a request with an explanation as to why it is reasonable.

The second step is for the other parent to say "yes" to reasonable requests. My general philosophy is to encourage parents to say yes unless there is a significant reason to say no when requests for temporary and reasonable modifications to the schedule are made. As mentioned above, it is quite likely that each of you will be making requests of the other parent over the years, and if both parents maintain this philosophy, conflict for your children will be reduced.

As described earlier, it is hoped that the parenting plan covers most of the necessary details. However, in the absence of a parenting plan, or if one parent questions some provision, conflicts may occur. Typically, things that lead to conflict may include the following:

- Starting and ending times of holidays
- Vacations
- Extracurricular activities

- School field trips, and who is going with the child
- New spouse/significant other
- Parenting philosophy
- School
- Costs for the children's activities and non-emergency medical and dental care
- Religious issues and schooling

As you think about each of these issues — and others that are particular to you and your ex-spouse — you might consider how to use your parenting plan to help prevent conflicts.

For example, if vacations are a source of conflict, your parenting plan might include the following:

"Each parent can have the children for two separate ten-day vacations during the summer break from school. Both parents are to submit vacation plans to the other parent no later than April 1st of each calendar year. Unless there is a conflict in dates, all vacation plans should automatically be approved. In the case of a dispute regarding dates, mother gets first choice of dates in even numbered years and father has first choice of dates in odd-numbered years."

By having this in the parenting plan, you will no longer need to argue about who gets what particular block of time for a vacation, or how long the vacation should be. Obviously, you will want to tailor the plan to match your particular circumstances.

Managing Extra Expenses for Your Child

Another troublesome issue for many parents seems to be clothing and the costs of extracurricular activities. Later, in chapter 6, I'll detail my opinion that clothing purchased for a child is the property of the child; it hurts the child when parents argue about where a particular piece of clothing is or who paid for it. Both parents should assist in purchasing adequate clothing, and each parent should have an adequate supply of clothing in his or her household, including underwear, pajamas, socks, and personal toiletry items. It is important not to hoard your child's clothing, often a problem with parents of very young children. As children get older, it is much easier for your child to simply make sure that the clothing they need is adequate in each home.

Unfortunately, it is all too common for parents to argue about finances when they do not have an adequate parenting plan. The following are two examples of things parents often say when there is not a reasonable agreement about sharing costs and expenses are as follows:

- "It's okay with me if you want to play little league, but your dad's going to have to pay for it since I don't have the money."
- "Piano lessons are a great idea. Tell your mother to pay for it because I give her $400 a month in child support. She can take it out of that support."

Regarding the costs of clothing or extracurricular activities, some parents believe that just because they pay child support they should not have to share in any other expenses. If you and the other parent argue about who will be paying for clothing, little league, or music lessons, your child will feel that your fight about money is more important than he is. In most states, child support is about equalizing the income available to the parents for raising the child. It covers the basics, such as housing and food. Both parents need to support their children's interests, so both parents should share in paying for these extracurricular activities. Again, the best way to handle this is to have an established formula in the parenting plan. An example of this could be as follows:

> *"Both parents are to share the cost of agreed-upon extra-curricular activities and all medical/dental expenses that are not covered by health insurance. Recognizing that there is a difference in the income between the parents, and that child support is being paid by father to mother to help equalize income, it is agreed that father will pay fifty-five percent of these costs and mother will pay forty-five percent of these costs. All other day-to-day expenses associated with raising the children will be paid by each parent during the time that the children are in his/her care."*

While there may be some disagreement as to which extra-curricular activities are agreed-upon, at least a formula will be in place for how to adjust the costs. Many parents are successful in managing this by keeping a tally of paid expenses that fall into this category. On a quarterly basis they submit their expense sheets to each other, and one parent pays the other to equalize the expenses according to the parenting plan. If both parents are diligent in this regard, your child's participation in activities will be more enjoyable and she will not feel in the middle of your conflicts.

Knowing When to Hold Firm

As I indicated earlier, it is important to know when to hold your ground and when to go along with the other parent. Parenting plans can help alleviate a lot of problems, but they require parents to follow the court order and the parenting plan. Parents must communicate in a business-like fashion and keep the child's needs in mind first. When parents are operating in good faith — caring more about the children than their conflict — they can plan ahead in order to resolve conflicts.

Unfortunately, there are some parents who simply want to fight, and when you are dealing with such a person, it becomes important to hold your ground. At the very highest levels of conflict, or when there are issues of substance abuse, domestic violence, or alienation of children, a well-defined parenting plan may help, but it may not be sufficient to resolve conflicts and keep your children out of the middle. When issues involve the safety and well-being of your children, your philosophy must change. You need to hold firm in your conviction and refuse to allow your child to become involved in situations that are damaging or dangerous. These issues and a process for reducing their negative effects will be discussed in chapters 9 and 10.

Things to Remember

Determine Your Level of Conflict

- If you are in low-to-medium conflict, you can probably co-parent and resolve most differences rather easily and in a way that avoids blame and anger and putting your child in the middle.

- If you are in a moderate level of conflict much of the time, you'll probably need to develop a business-like style of communication, learn to disengage from conflict, and develop a parenting plan that is very detailed and thorough.

- For some families, there are more significant problems that cannot be solved in this way. When the level of conflict is quite high, one parent seems to enjoy arguing and controlling the other parent, or there are concerns about abuse, alienation, violence, or other significant problems, you will need additional assistance. This will be discussed more fully in chapter 9.

Learn the Appropriate Style of Parenting

- Is co-operative or parallel parenting the right style for your relationship? Select the style which is most appropriate based on the level of conflict you and your ex- have chosen to live with, be sure to learn how to make it work in the best interests of your child(ren).

Develop a Thorough Parenting Plan

- With a thorough and detailed parenting plan, you'll probably be able to resolve all of your issues without going to court and without much aggravation, as long as both of you abide by it. If necessary, use mediation to develop your parenting plan. (More about mediation in chapter 9.)

Your Child Is Not a Percentage

How to Share Your Child

"No person was ever honored for what he received; honor has been awarded for what he gave."
— Calvin Coolidge

Crystal's parents divorced when she was six, and for the first two years after the breakup, they argued over everything. By the time Crystal was eight, things had settled down. She lived with her mother, and saw her father every other weekend. Crystal was adjusting reasonably well to this routine. However, her father was frustrated that he never got to help Crystal with her schooling, and felt like a "Disneyland Dad." He wanted more time with her. He also realized that he was paying more child support because he only had Crystal for about thirty percent of the time. Wanting to be an equal parent he went back to court to get "50-50" custody. This started a new battle and Crystal became sad, scared, and insecure. Both parents were pressuring her to choose where to live. Her mother wanted to retain primary custody, and her father wanted to be an equal parent. What had been a reasonable parenting plan was ruined for Crystal because her parents lost their ability to share time with her.

INCREASINGLY, PARENTS ARE SEEKING joint physical custody of their children, many wanting to have their children with them "equally." In all of my work with families of divorce, the phrase I hear most often, and which causes parents and those who work with high-conflict families the greatest frustration, is "I want 50-50 with my child." These parents are referring to the desire for their children to live with them half of the time. It is common for parents to come to their evaluation describing the amount of time that they have with their child as a percentage, such as, "I have my son twenty-four percent of the time," rather than saying, "I have my son every other weekend and one night per week."

When you think of your time with your child as a percentage, it appears as if you think of your child as an object. The underlying issue for many parents is that they do not believe they can share their children unless they have *equal* "possession," "influence" and "parenting time." In my opinion, this places tremendous burden on children and increases loyalty conflicts. Before Crystal's parents started to fight over parenting time, she was doing fine. Now that they're fighting, she is depressed and insecure. She wants her parents to be happy, and she can't please them both. She feels a need to be "fair" to both of her parents. The position she's in isn't good for her. It will cause her to focus more on pleasing her parents instead of just being a child!

This chapter offers parents a different way of sharing children regardless of the amount of time have with the children. The key is to *participate in your child's life in a meaningful way.* Parents who take part in all aspects of their children's lives and who remain actively involved need not worry about percentages. They maintain a healthy relationship with their children and avoid placing their children in the middle of conflict.

In fact, many parents think that their children need an *equal* relationship with both of them. However, research in the past several years suggests that children benefit from quality time with their children spent in a wide range of their children's life experience and activities.[1] Michael Lamb, who used to work at the National Institute of Mental Health, has described that this means children benefit when both of their parents spend at least 30–35% of the time with them, *distributed well.* This means that the actual percentage of time is less important than the way in which that time is distributed. Distributing the time well allows each parent to have the quality relationship that children need and that most parents want when they get divorced.

Building a Relationship with Your Child

Relationships are not built on the *quantity* of time, but the *quality* of the time that is spent with parents and children together. I've seen parents who have their child only in the summer and have a healthier relationship with their child than another parent who has his child almost every day during the school year. Many adolescents in long-distance situations yearn to be with the other parent in order to grow in their relationship with the parent who has been absent for much of their lives. By focusing on the importance of your relationship with your child, you can provide quality nurturing, guidance, affection, and support whether you have your child twenty-five percent or seventy-five percent of the time. (It can be difficult — but certainly not impossible — to build a relationship if you have your child with you less than twenty percent of the time.)

Most importantly, if you focus on your relationship with your child, and not your percentage of time, you will give your child a message that she is important. When you are focused on your child's activities, feelings, and needs rather than your rights, needs, and demands, she will feel valued, nurtured, and supported. Communicate with your child, and listen to and understand her feelings.

There is no doubt that your child has a need for a healthy, intact, relationship with both her parents, as long as both of you are healthy role models for her. This will require you to share your time in such a way that there is frequent contact with both of you. If you're like many parents, you will want to meet your child's developmental needs and support his interests. Many parents think about their child's day-to-day needs and work out a timeshare that incorporates these day-to-day needs and the ability of each parent to meet them.

Understanding your daughter's developmental needs and working together will guarantee her psychological and physical development will progress in a smooth, healthy manner. Don't be concerned about how much time you have with her, instead, focus on how to help her grow, and provide her with positive and loving care, sharing her in a way that maximizes her relationship with each parent. Crystal and her parents were doing that before they started arguing over the "percentage" of time. This might mean you will only have your child every other weekend, yet the relationship between you and your child will continue to grow. Take pride and comfort in knowing that your daughter is doing well and that you've had a positive role in her development.

> In contrast to Crystal, Tiffany's parents initially shared the time with her on a relatively equal basis from the time she was eight until she was twelve. While the parents lived in communities about fifteen minutes apart, Tiffany went to school in her mother's community, and her father transported Tiffany to and from school during her time with him. Both parents participated in Tiffany's activities, which included soccer and music lessons, and felt relatively good about the equal nature of their caregiving.

However, as Tiffany was ready to enter middle school, both of her parents realized that Tiffany's need for consistency and structure in a single household outweighed the need for equal parenting time. Additionally, both parents wished to move, and the communities they were looking at were about a half-hour apart, which would make it difficult for them to share the time equally. In spite of the fact that these parents were used to arguing over every detail of Tiffany's life, they reached the same conclusion: namely, that the healthiest parenting arrangement would be for Tiffany to spend primary time in one house and more limited time in the other house.

Mediation helped them to resolve their differences and arrange a schedule in which Tiffany was with her father during the school week, and her mother every other weekend and most of the summer. During the summer, the basic schedule was reversed, and Tiffany lived with her mother and stayed with her father on alternate weekends. Both of Tiffany's parents felt good about the *quality* of their ongoing relationships, even though there was a drastic change in the *quantity* of time that Tiffany was with each of them. This is the kind of example in which their child's developmental needs (an opportunity to build friendships and a support system in one community) outweighed the parents' desire for equal time.

Jamie, an eighteen-month-old, has parents who argue over every minute of time. Her father wants equal time and demands that Jamie be with each of them on an alternating-week schedule. He is asserting his right to be an equal parent and Jamie's need for frequent and continuing contact with both of them. Since they live approximately forty-five minutes apart, he believes that the best way to share Jamie is to exchange her every week and then each of them will be able to parent her.

Unfortunately, this will present a developmental dilemma for Jamie. Child development experts recognize that children under the age of two require considerable consistency between their caregivers, and communication about their child's important day-to-day needs. While research now supports that children can become attached to two (or even three) caregivers, they often do so within the context of one household, one routine, and one primary parent, while the other caregiver usually takes a somewhat secondary role. Even in families in which both parents are together, most young children receive the primary care from one of the two parents. The other parent, while very important in the child's growth and development, usually has a less-than-equal role. Research supports that children benefit from both of their parents, and that both parents tend to contribute differently to their child's well-being. However, research does not support the belief that children need both parents equally and that they benefit from *equal* time with divorced parents.

Your child's developmental needs are most important following your separation. If you can work toward meeting his developmental needs, and defer your own needs and rights, there is a greater likelihood that he will grow up to have healthy relationships with both of you. As we will discuss further in chapter 4, very young children usually do better in one primary household with considerable contact with the other parent. This often will include overnight access with both parents if the child is emotionally equipped to handle it. If Jamie's father would put aside his fear of losing a relationship with her and allow for a more gradual transition to relatively equal time, it is likely that the relationship itself will be stronger when Jamie is four or five. Chapter 4 will focus more on your child's developmental needs and what it takes to make joint physical custody work with younger children.

It's important for you to keep a perspective of the long-term well-being of your child rather than the short-term inequities of time on which many parents seem so focused. Remember that your *relationship* with your child is more critical than the actual amount of *time* you spend with your child.

Parenting Regardless of the Time Share

Parenting requires a variety of skills, and skills vary according to the developmental needs of the child. Very young children have basic daily needs that include nurturing, affection, food, and a consistent routine. They need relationships from which they can develop and work out their separation and autonomy — growing independence and sense of "self" — as they move into their toddler years. In addition to the basics, toddlers need an ongoing routine, emotional support, socialization, and the freedom to explore their environment in a safe and secure manner. School-age children need all of the above, and assistance with school work, support for their recreational activities, growth in their friendships, guidance, and an environment in which they can feel loved, supported, and nurtured. Adolescents need rules, structure, guidance, continued educational and social support, and relationships in which they can explore issues associated with their identity, their future, and their role in society. They need to be respected for their desires and needs relating to their time-sharing plan. They need help with feelings about dating and sexuality, driving, applying to college, learning a skill or trade, and other basic essentials in their ongoing development toward adulthood.

Whether you are co-parenting or parallel parenting (see chapter 2), the task is to share in all of your child's needs. It doesn't necessarily mean sharing equally, nor does it mean that two different parents will perform these tasks equally well. Obviously, fathers cannot nurse their infants, but both parents can change diapers, feed, toilet train, nurture, and cuddle. In many families, one parent may be better at providing guidance and structure and listening, while the other parent may be better at understanding the child's feelings. One parent may be very organized and able to assist in scheduling the child's many activities, while the other parent may be a good teacher or coach, or be more successful at helping with homework. Ideally, both parents will share activities in such a way that they can complement each other, each performing a variety of tasks, but most importantly, performing the task that each does best.

In a non-divorced household, children typically have an opportunity to benefit from the strengths of each parent, and each parent tends to buffer the child from the weaknesses of the other parent. For example, if you are the parent who is better connected to your child's emotions, he is more likely to come to you when he feels sad. At the same time, if you get stressed and have an outburst (as all parents do once in a while), the other parent may tell your son, "Don't worry, Mom's had a bad day. Let's go do something and give her some time to rest."

In contrast, children of divorce rarely have parents who support each other in that way. It is important for you to recognize your own individual strengths and weaknesses and not get into competition with your child's other parent. You don't need to parent better than the other parent, just the best that you can. It's important for you to support the other parent for your children, even when the other parent makes mistakes. Just because you're divorced doesn't mean that you should avoid buffering your child from the other parent's stresses. Don't exploit minor problems with the other parent for your benefit.

For example, if your child comes home from time with her dad and says that he was angry all weekend, you don't want to say something like, "I'm not surprised, he always got mad at me when I didn't do what he wanted." A more appropriate response would be to say, "You know, all of us get mad sometimes. Any idea why he was having a rough weekend? Do you want to talk about it?" At the same time, I encourage parents to add the following: "I'm glad you feel comfortable telling me when you're upset, no matter who you're upset with. I hope you told your dad that you were upset, and I sure hope you'll tell me when you're upset with me." By doing this, you encourage your child to share her feelings and you give her the message that all parents make mistakes sometimes. This can help generalize any frustration that she's feeling. In this way, you are emotionally buffering her frustration with her dad, rather than promoting it.

If each of you works to parent your children, either together or individually, you can both actively participate in a wide range of tasks and activities with your children, regardless of the amount of time you actually spend with your children.

Supporting Your Child's Time and Relationship with the Other Parent

It is critical for both parents to support the child's relationship with the other parent. Rather than becoming territorial, trying to do everything yourself, and acting as if the other parent doesn't exist, it is important to honor your child's relationship with the other parent. When fourteen-year-old Jillian and her mother are talking about dating, it's important for Jillian's mother to suggest that she talk with her father about it as well. This encourages Jillian's relationship with her father and gives Jillian the message that Mom values Dad's input to the discussion. Similarly, when Jane, age four, wakes up from a nightmare at Dad's house, and he spends time cuddling and soothing her back to sleep, it's important that Dad encourages Jane to talk with Mom about her nightmare later that day.

If your child is feeling insecure, it's very important to encourage him to go to the other parent for support. For example, if Timmy is upset about not making the soccer team, it's important for Mom to enlist Dad's assistance in helping him feel better. It may very well be that Dad is better equipped to support his feelings, and Mom needs to accept this. Don't try to do everything. Your child has two parents, and *both* of you need to share the parenting tasks. When you do, you show your child that you support and encourage your child's time and relationship with the other parent. If you work together, whether you are co-parenting or parallel parenting, you are working in a complementary way *for the benefit of your child.*

The two of you aren't equal in your parenting interests and abilities, so don't try to be. You might be more artistic, so take your son to museums, the theater, and art shows. Encourage his participation in music lessons. Consider yourself the "cultural parent" and stimulate those interests. Are you more of an outdoor person? If so, take him on hikes, bicycle trips, or camping. Consider yourself the "outdoor fun parent." However, don't try to take over the other parent's pursuits. If you know that the other parent is a good coach and has encouraged your son's participation in sports from an early age, enjoy watching your son's games from the sidelines and consider the other parent the "athletic parent."

While each of you might have interests that are unique, there may be others that you will share. Both of you can promote your child to improve his reading, take him to the library, and help him with his homework. Both of you can share in the field trips, perhaps alternating them or choosing by the activity. Both of you might take him on vacations to interesting places and to meet family and friends. Don't compete with each other on these shared activities. Take pleasure in promoting your relationship together.

Most of all, don't sit back and do nothing just because the other parent is active in some areas. Think about your own interests and share them with your child. That's a part of what parenting is all about, and can happen regardless of the amount of time you share together!

What to Do When Your Time is Limited

In your situation, the luxury of sufficient quality time with your children may not be possible. Whether due to a court order which limits your time, or due to a long-distance relationship, you may be removed from the daily life of your children. In these circumstances, building a relationship requires more planning and care.

Your most important ingredient in building a relationship limited by time or distance is regular and consistent contact with your child. Regular phone calls serve as an opportunity to show your child that you care and that you are interested in her daily life. Send pictures, audio, or video tapes by mail. Sending a fax or e-mail shows that you love her and are committed to staying in touch. If your child is quite young, "out of sight" could become "out of mind." She will have a hard time feeling loved and connected if you maintain little or no contact between your face-to-face contacts. It is essential that you keep your contact regular and consistent so that your child feels a strong connection to you, even though you may be distant.

You can also show your child that you care by asking about her life and staying connected to her activities. Talk with your child's teacher, and let your child know about the conversation that you've had. One father I know who lived a thousand miles from his son talked with his son's teacher on a weekly basis, and then talked with his son about those phone calls. His son felt loved and important.

If you are in the same community, but don't have frequent access, go to the parent-teacher conferences and share the information that you learned with your child. Show interest and attend sporting events, music recitals, or other activities that your child participates in. Your daughter won't understand when you say you want frequent visitation and then don't watch her soccer games on the weekends that she is with you. This will frustrate her and make her feel that you're not involved in her life.

Maintaining Your Relationship over a Long Distance

If you live in another city, it is even more important to maintain consistent contact. It's easy for children to feel disconnected from parents who live far away, so it is important for you to take the initiative in the relationship. Remember that it is *your job* to be present in your child's life as much as possible. Whenever possible, visit your child on special weekends or for special school or extracurricular events. Even one trip per year to your child's city for a special event helps your child feel special and know that you care. Maintain regular and consistent visits, and attempt to see your child at least every three months.

In the past several years, several states[2] have legislatively supported what is referred to as "virtual visitation." While no one would say that virtual visitation is the same as direct and regular contact, the concept is better than limited or no contact. Such legislation recognizes the need for regular contact between parents and their children. Judges are now making orders that encourage the use of emails, the use of video cameras to work on a child's homework, regular phone calls, and the use of other technologies to maintain such access. The purpose of this legislation is to ensure that parents and children have the most possible contact in between face-to-face access and to encourage parents who live a long-distance from their children to stay directly involved in their child's life.

Just because you live far away doesn't mean you should feel sorry for yourself and withdraw. Take a proactive role and find out what you can do for your child. When her teacher tells you that your daughter loves painting in class, buy her an art kit and encourage her to send you drawings. Send her a book about art museums appropriate for her age. If you have e-mail and Internet access, send her the Internet address of your favorite museum. When you visit each other, don't miss the opportunity to share even more in that interest. All of this was made possible by a simple phone call with her teacher and your creative follow-through.

Children who live farther away from their parents often have extended visitation during school holidays and summer vacations, and it is important to use the time with your child to build your relationship. Participate in child-focused activities, encourage your child to make friends in your neighborhood, and truly get to know your child. While a long-distance relationship is difficult, it is very important for your child to maintain the relationship with you. If you are generally absent in your child's life, it can be very painful for both of you. While children might have trouble adjusting to a long-distance relationship, they have much more difficulty adjusting to feeling abandoned when a long-distance parent becomes absent. For yourself and your child, it is important to maintain and build your relationship as much as possible, no matter how difficult the logistics may be.

If you are the primary custodial parent, your task may also be difficult. If you are like many divorced parents, it may seem easier for you when the other parent has limited contact with your child. But if the other parent withdraws, you will have to deal with your child's feelings of abandonment. Be smart and creative and support your child with the logistics of a long-distance relationship. Do this because you love him. Encourage him to call his other parent, and share his interests and activities. Send copies of school information, including the teacher's names, phone numbers and email addresses, to the other parent and inform the other parent of your child's interests and activities. Keep a journal of your child's life and send a copy of it monthly to the other parent. This will allow the parent to have the necessary information for building a relationship with your child. If you keep the other parent informed, it is less likely your child will feel caught in the middle of your divorce. Most importantly, when you share this information and encourage your child to develop and maintain a relationship with the long-distance parent, your child feels better about himself and knows that your love for him is greater than your anger at the other parent.

Your child may long for a more connected relationship with the distant parent as she approaches adolescence. When that occurs, she may also want to move to the other parent's home during the school year. I have often seen children entering adolescence who have missed the connection with their long-distance parent, and view this as the best time to build that relationship. As they are forming their own independence, and making moves to break away from their parental bond, such children will seek to strengthen the other relationship before moving into adulthood. Children who do this seem to recognize that it is their final chance to truly build a more complete parent-child relationship with a long-distance parent.

If you are the primary custodial parent, this may mean letting go of your child before you are prepared to. Most parents recognize that their children will move on after graduation from high school, usually around age eighteen. It feels premature if your child wants to leave home at age fourteen or fifteen so that she can go live with and develop a relationship with the other parent. As difficult as this may be for you, if your child requests to make such a switch, it will be very important for your child and her overall development. Sometimes the most loving and unselfish gift you can give your child is the freedom to build the relationship with a parent who has been more or less absent in her life.

Obviously, such a move is a very critical and important undertaking. You might find it best to consult with a therapist who understands these issues. Consultation may be an important step in determining whether or not you should consider the change of custody. Try to understand your child's motives and look at it through her eyes. This will help you understand the potential benefit of such a change. If your child moves and you become the long-distance parent, it is important to maintain your relationship with your child, utilizing the methods described earlier in this chapter.

Sample Calendar Arrangements

Take a look at these sample calendar arrangements that many parents use to develop parenting plans. Keep in mind that any one of these might be good for your family; you might need to try several until you find the one that works best. When your children are younger, use a large calendar in each home that is color-coded to help them identify where they will be going. As they grow, this helps them plan activities and let friends know where they will be. Keep in mind your child's needs will change as she gets older, and your schedule might need to be adjusted. If you talk and listen to your child, you will hopefully find a schedule that balances your lifestyles with your child's needs.

Each of these calendar segments will reflect a four-week cycle. You will notice a pattern to them, and they should be repeated. While I may designate Mom (M) or Dad (D) in different time slots, remember that it's the child's welfare that is important, not the needs of either parent. (Holidays and other adjustments are discussed more fully in chapter 2.)

Primary Parent Schedule
(Preferable if before the divorce your child had one primary parent or you were never married and there has been a paternity action, so that you have not spent much time with your child)

This schedule will provide your child frequent and continuing contact with both parents. With a very young child, rather than one midweek overnight, consider a Tuesday and Thursday dinner visit, reserving overnights for the weekends.

Monday	Tuesday	Wednesday	Thursday	Friday	Saturday	Sunday
M	M	D	M	M	M	M
M	M	D	M	D	D	D
M	M	D	M	M	M	M
M	M	D	M	D	D	D

If you have a very young child (less than twelve months) and one primary parent, you will probably want to start by gradually increasing her time with the other parent. You might introduce four-hour blocks of time with the other parent to play and nurture the child, gradually increasing to six- or eight-hour blocks of time. These should probably be at least every third day, if possible. On weekends, you might consider two days in a row as a way of emphasizing the developing relationship. Then, as you find that your child is comfortable with the other parent, and comfortable with being away from you, you can introduce overnights. As your child gets older, and certainly by the time he reaches age three, your child can probably adjust to one of the plans described below (either 3-4-4-3 or traditional).

3-4-4-3 Schedule
(Generally good for a younger child with two relatively equal homes and a temperament that can tolerate overnights. This schedule requires good communication between the parents.)

Monday	Tuesday	Wednesday	Thursday	Friday	Saturday	Sunday
M	M	M	D	D	D	D
M	M	M	M	D	D	D
M	M	M	D	D	D	D
M	M	M	M	D	D	D

2-2-5-5 Schedule
(Good for school-aged or adolescent children with two relatively equal homes and a desire to spend equal time with each parent. For many children, it can be better than a week-week schedule, since they are never away from either parent for longer than five days. Additionally, such a schedule allows each parent to each participate in activities with the child on a weekly basis, such as a special art class on Thursday for dad and his daughter, or a special mother-daughter dance class on Monday.)

Monday	Tuesday	Wednesday	Thursday	Friday	Saturday	Sunday
M	M	D	D	M	M	M
M	M	D	D	D	D	D
M	M	D	D	M	M	M
M	M	D	D	D	D	D

Week — Week Schedule
(Good for equal parenting plans and children who can tolerate a full week away from each parent. Some parents schedule a midweek dinner or overnight visit with the other parent, but for some children this can be more disruptive than the 2-2-5-5 schedule above.)

Monday	Tuesday	Wednesday	Thursday	Friday	Saturday	Sunday
M	M	M	M	M	M	M
D	D	D	D	D	D	D
M	M	M	M	M	M	M
D	D	D	D	D	D	D

School-Year / Summer Schedule

When parents live in separate communities it can be difficult to plan a schedule. If you have a long-distance relationship, your child will need to be in one home during the school year, and visit the other parent during non-school time. Consider the travel time and your child's age and activities when you develop your schedule. If you are the "summer parent," try and spend some time with your child every three months. If your child is young, you might need to do most of the traveling. Many parents are reluctant to have their child fly alone, especially with the added stressors of traveling these days, even if the airlines allow it. If you are able to arrange non-stop flights, it will be easier than if your child has to change planes. Once you decide that your child is old enough to travel by himself, it's still important to come visit him at least once or twice a year. Use three-day weekends for monthly contact during the school year if you live close enough, or longer holiday breaks such as Thanksgiving or Easter if you live farther away.

If you are the "school year parent" and live a long distance from the other parent, try and enroll your child in a year-round school. This allows for more frequent travel to be with the other parent, yet won't take her away for as long as the traditional summer break. Consider the logistics in both communities, since working parents need daycare or planned activities when children come to visit. Your child is likely to do well if she has all but one week of each break with the long-distance parent. That leaves her some time to be with friends in her home community and time for vacation trips with each parent.

If your child is in a typical school-year/summer-vacation schedule, she is likely to have two weeks of vacation at Christmas, another week or two during the spring or near Easter, and about twelve weeks off in the summer. If she's under age eight, consider having an equal split of the Christmas break, and most spring breaks with the long-distance parent. Try breaking up the summer into three segments: the first and third with the long-distance parent and the middle one with the home parent. This may prevent her from feeling homesick during her trips. If she's older and used to being away from home, she might do well spending most of the summer with the long-distance parent, assuming she enjoys it there and has a good relationship with that parent. Both of you need to consider her interests, summer camp desires, and vacation needs as you develop your plan.

Finally, it's important to know that many children whose parents live in two different communities grow to resent the travel. Talk to your child about the travel, and look for positive ways to manage the relationship. If you think that your child is tiring of the travel, consider doing more of it yourself. A change of custody, even if just for a couple of years, might help your child feel a sense of belonging in both communities. You might also consider using mediation or an evaluation (more on this in chapter 9) to help you if you can't decide together how to manage long-distance visits. This is especially helpful if your child is reluctant to share his feelings about the travel because he's afraid of hurting your feelings. Talking with your child about his feelings will help him know that you care about him and help him make the adjustment to your lives in separate cities.

Things to Remember

This chapter has focused on ways to build a relationship with your children — even if you don't have equal time with them:

- participating in their activities,
- maintaining frequent contact,
- sharing in their daily lives.

Even if you have a long-distance relationship with your children, you can maintain and improve your relationship through such technological devices as:

- frequent phone calls
- faxes
- e-mail
- a video camera
- blogs

- text messaging
- MySpace, YouTube, and similar online resources.

Parenting is not about the amount of time you spend with your children, but how you relate to them, understand them and support their needs, share yourself, and guide them as they grow! Look in chapter 4 for more on your child's developmental needs.

Notes

[1] See e.g., Lamb, M. E., Sternberg, K. J., & Thompson, R. A. The Effects of Divorce and Custody Arrangements on Children's Behavior, Development, and Adjustment, *Family and Conciliation Courts Review*, Vol. 35, No. 4, pgs. 393–404, 1997.

[2] Utah, for example.

CHAPTER 4

Your Child's Childhood

Developmental Needs
Through the Years

*"Safeguarding the rights of others is the most noble and
beautiful end of a human being."*
— Kahlil Gibran

IF YOU ARE LIKE MOST PARENTS, you're likely to wonder
how your divorce will affect your child. Like many life experiences,
the effect is dependent upon many factors, but especially the age
of the child. It's obvious that infants and toddlers need a different
style of parenting than adolescents. Similarly, a two-year-old may react
differently to the birth of a sibling than a seven-year-old will.

In the same way, divorce will affect a very young child quite
differently than an older child. This chapter is designed to focus on
children's developmental needs, that is, their needs at different ages.
I have divided this chapter into four major age groups. Keep in mind
there may be an overlap between children of close ages, even if they
are in different groups. Also, many children regress — revert to earlier
or more infantile patterns — when parents divorce because of the
initial anxiety and insecurity they feel. It is common for children to
regress for a short period of time. Paying attention to the information
given for younger age groups — as well as that of your own child's —
may help you better understand your child and his needs. If your child
regresses for more than six months, you are likely to need the help of
a therapist.

In this chapter, I'll explain the basic characteristics, behavior, and
needs of children within each age group. We'll also explore how
divorce affects children at different ages, and I'll suggest some ways
you can help your child adjust to your divorce.

Many parents wonder about what residential arrangements are
"best" for their children. If you have read books on divorce, you
might notice some debate within the mental health community about

this very issue. Research suggests that your mental health and how much conflict your child is exposed to are more important variables in determining how your child will adjust to your divorce than the visitation schedule. If the circumstances are right, even very young children can adjust to two homes. Many school-age children need the consistency of one home, while others need the consistency of both parents actively involved in their life. Regardless of your schedule, your child may have trouble if he is exposed to too much conflict.

Just a reminder: the schedule which works best is unique to your particular family and lifestyle. I urge you to develop your specific parenting plan — with the help of a mediator if necessary — according to your child's needs and your family's lifestyle and circumstances.

Infants and Toddlers (0–3 years)

During these first three years of life, the foundations of basic trust and relationships are formed. Research in the past 10 years has shown that children form attachments with both of their parents, usually about the same time (age 6–7 months). Prior to that, they connect with anyone who is meeting their day-to-day needs, but they begin to differentiate strangers from close care-takers as the attachment deepens. While there are often clear differences in how mothers and fathers interact with their very young children (for example mothers tend to hold and soothe and fathers tend to engage in more active play), and many children have a preference for one or the other parent, attachment with both parents is important. This is because children benefit from the different styles of interactions that they receive from both mothers and fathers.

By the end of the first year, language skills are developing. Your infant's personality is forming and your child is learning to trust you and sense that the world is a secure place. During the toddler years, your child begins developing her own sense of self, and starts to separate from her parents. She will begin to assert herself. Her emotions may become unpredictable. This age is often referred to as "the terrible two's," because many children in this age group have temper outbursts, frequently say "no," and may be demanding and stubborn. However, these behaviors are very important for your child's development. Your child's behaviors — and your responses to her behaviors — will set the stage for her self-esteem and future relationships. By age three, if all goes well, these emotions settle down, language skills are more advanced, and she is likely to be toilet trained and interacting more easily with strangers and other children.

Children in this age group require predictability, consistency, and routine. If her parents have never lived together, there may be no adjustment when an infant spends a couple of nights in each parent's home. This may simply feel quite natural and may reflect "normalcy" for her.

However, when parents have lived together and a divorce occurs during this time, there is a loss which your child feels but cannot fully comprehend. This loss can be extreme if there is a major disruption in the consistency of the existing relationships. She may express frustration through her behavior and emotions. Typical symptoms include regression and developmental delays. Your child may experience problems with feeding, sleeping, and self-soothing. Some children become irritable, depressed, and withdrawn, in part because they don't know how to express their loss in words. Separation anxiety for children in this age group may increase. If one or both parents become depressed — a common occurrence — basic care may diminish.

Rather than the idea of one "psychological parent," or "primary parent," recent research reveals that children have more than one important attachment figure. As noted above, children develop their attachment with both parents around the same age. However, if one of you has been the parent your child is most attached to, and looks to when she is feeling insecure or needy, some may consider you the "primary parent." If your child is equally comfortable going to you and her other parent when she is hungry, hurting, or insecure, most will consider that you are both "primary parents." Still other children may have even three adults — such as two parents and a grandparent or day-care provider — who are relatively equal at meeting their day-to-day needs. While your child's needs may be similar regardless of this, children of this age will benefit from a range of parenting plan options based in part on the nature of their attachments and other issues in their life. With very young children, it is often helpful to arrange the post-divorce parenting plan to be relatively close to the pre-divorce parenting plan, at least for the first few months of the divorce as a way of reducing adjustment problems. At the same time, it will be important for both of you to be actively involved in a wide variety of your child's life experiences and activities. That usually means that neither of you will be away from your child for more than two or three days at a time and that both of you will be involved in feeding routines, sleep routines, active play and quieter nurturing.

Parenting plans for children of this age group need to integrate the following ideas:

• Your child's relationship with the primary parent or parents is most important during the first three years of life.

• The critical task for infants in the first year of life is to develop a healthy attachment to a parent or both parents. This attachment serves as the foundation for future relationships. Absence from either parent for too long a period of time (more than 3 days) is often detrimental to the formation of such attachments because, for children under age 3, out of sight is out of mind.

• Research on day-care shows that children can develop normally when separated from parents who are at work, suggesting that very young children can tolerate regular separations from one parent to be with the other parent. This will be affected by how much each parent has been directly involved in the child's life.

• If there is only one primary parent, frequent, shorter visits with the other parent may be ideal in the first year to eighteen months. Overnight visits may need to be limited in the first year of life if there is only one primary parent. On the other hand, if your child is attached relatively equally to both of you, there does not appear to be any particular problems with overnights in both homes. In fact, your child is likely to benefit from overnights in each home as a way of strengthening the attachment with each of you.

• The major role of parents and care-givers is to provide security, love, support, flexibility, and consistency.

• As your child's mental development allows him to hold memories of you when you are not with him, he may begin to tolerate and benefit from more overnight time with the other parent. Depending on your child's temperament and other factors discussed below, this may shift between 18–36 months.

• Sharing the parenting equally will require that your child has an easy enough temperament and can adjust to changes in routine rather easily. Such children are neither very shy, nor considered to be demanding or difficult. They are basically easy-going in their attitude. You and the other parent will need to support each other and exchange your child without conflict. You will need similar routines in each household, relative stability of the transitions, and an ability to communicate about your child's developmental, medical, and emotional needs. It will be important to arrange a plan that allows both of you to help with these needs.

- If direct communication is difficult for the two of you, the use of a parenting notebook, in which each of you write important information about your child and her needs can be quite helpful. Use the book to write about soothing techniques, emerging language, foods she is enjoying or avoiding, sleep routines, health issues, and other day-to-day issues in the life of your child.

Regardless of the schedule, your child benefits when the two of you help each other understand your young child, work together to develop routines that are familiar to your child, cooperate on soothing your child, help each other as your child starts talking, reassure each other in your respective parenting techniques, and learn to be flexible as your child grows and changes. This style of communication occurs in healthy, intact families. If used in your separated family, a shared parenting plan will be natural for you and your child.

On the other hand, if you are in a great deal of conflict with the other parent, your very young child may benefit from a schedule that is similar to your pre-separation life. You may want to continue the time and caregiving arrangements you had prior to separation. From your child's viewpoint, there is no need to have either of you considered the primary parent in the legal system; rather, your child needs to rely on the predictability of his environment until your conflict subsides. More than anything, avoid conflict in front of your child and at transitions and use the parent communication notebook to enhance your understanding of your child when he is at the other parent's home.

Preschoolers (3–5 years)

During this stage, children have a better ability to understand language, relationships, and feelings. Children of this age develop their thinking skills and increase their friendships. If the attachment and separation process has been healthy, children can go to preschool rather easily and start to make friends. Children in this age group are delightful! They are learning to understand and manage their feelings, and are fascinated about everything. If they have secure attachments with their parents and have received healthy parenting, they will be ready to go on to kindergarten with plenty of self-esteem and confidence.

On the other hand, preschoolers are at risk for fairly serious regression when they are feeling insecure about their relationships with their parents. Since they might not have the language skills to fully understand what is happening in their life, they can become easily confused and worry when a parental separation occurs. Developmental delays and regression in toileting, sleeping, and eating are common. Children may experience irritability and display clinging behavior. Some children become depressed and withdrawn. Nightmares may become more frequent or pronounced. Self-confidence may suffer and there can be an increase in aggressive and strange behaviors. Many children in this age group worry about their parents and may try to act "perfect" because they are afraid of the changes in their lives. They may also worry about their parents and try to take some responsibility for them, blaming themselves for adult problems. A certain amount of these behaviors are normal during the early stages of a separation or divorce, but too much regression or regression that lasts more than 6 months could reflect a more serious problem for your child.

Parenting plans for children of this age group need to cover these issues:

• Continued predictability, routine, and structure are important for the child.

• Children age three and older can generally benefit from overnight contact with each parent.

• Discipline and routine must be consistent in each parent's home. Recent research on parenting styles suggests that an *authoritative* parenting style is healthiest for children. Authoritative parenting combines structure, routine discipline, and guidance with nurturing attention to your child's feelings. This is in contrast to *authoritarian* parenting which is overly harsh and relatively unstructured parenting which is overly lax, neither of which is as positive as authoritative parenting.

• You will continue to need to share information about your child's eating, sleeping, toileting, medical, social, and emotional functioning.

• Your child needs freedom from direct conflict. If you continue to be in conflict with the other parent, you will need to consider using neutral sites for transitions (such as preschool or day-care). If you speak on the phone with the other parent, do so after your child is asleep, so he does not overhear any potentially unpleasant conversations.

• Children in this age group often benefit from blocks of time with each parent that enables them to settle into a routine at each home. Try to avoid frequent transitions. While younger children often benefit from more transitions, by the time a child is three or four years old, she can usually do well spending as many as three or four days away from either parent.

• Put your needs secondary to your child's. While one parent may want longer blocks of time as your child gets a bit older, some children in this age group may require more time in one home with a more consistent routine. Factors to consider are whether there has been a primary parent, whether you and the other parent are consistent and relatively free of conflict, and whether your child is experiencing significant stress.

• There may be situations where each of you will have some serious parenting difficulties. Even if that is the case, each of you can offer your child something the other cannot. You will want a parenting plan that maximizes the strengths of each parent, while minimizing the weaknesses. You will also want to work on improving your parenting to be more authoritative. There are excellent parenting programs and divorce education programs around the country to assist you with this. Look for such a program in your community, either through your court system or your local community college.

School-Age Children (6–12 years)

At this age, children thrive on structure and routine. Friendships grow and they improve skills in their social relationships. Many children of this age are very creative, and children in this group are good at making up games with unique rules. These rules are important as school-age children focus on fairness in their lives. Socialization and being part of a group are important to children of this age. They are learning to better understand and express their feelings and master academic skills. They can be quite silly at times, and still prefer to play much of the time. They learn skills in such areas as academics, sports, music, dance, and art. Self-esteem grows when they function well in school, on the playground, and in the family. Many children of this age have a different type of relationship with each parent, preferring Mom for some things and Dad for others.

Divorce brings many challenges to children of this age. Younger school-age children tend to feel the loss of the family as a unit and may experience sadness and crying. They may regress and seem more emotionally immature. Older children in this age group may be more likely to experience anger and choose one parent over the other as a way to hold onto their self-esteem and relationships. Your child may feel directly responsible for your divorce, especially if she is put in the middle of your conflict. Some children will exhibit more severe symptoms, including tantrums, regression, sleep problems, behavioral and academic problems in school, withdrawal from or aggression with peers, and depression. Some children are reluctant to grow up, remaining emotionally immature. Children in this age group believe in fairness and want to please their parents. They may feel overwhelmed by your conflicts and try to fix them, yet they can't. If one of you is depressed, your child may try to take care of you and help you with your emotional problems. When this happens, your child may become "parentified." This is not healthy for children, as parents are supposed to be taking care of their child's feelings and needs and not the other way around.

In extremely high-conflict families, children may have no obvious symptoms. They may feel overwhelmed and scared, but don't show anyone. These children are at risk for emotional splitting, where they perceive one parent is "all-good" and the other is "all-bad." Many children feel stuck by the loyalty conflicts between their parents and may keep their emotions inside, worrying about their parents. If your child was previously close with both of you, and now is only close to one of you, she may be feeling abandoned, confused, or alienated. Your child will have difficulty maintaining her self-image if you and the other parent are in very high conflict. Struggling with her emotions, your child may become emotionally overwhelmed and disorganized. I'll discuss the topic of alienated children in more detail in chapter 10.

It is common for children to hear one parent blame the other or hear different explanations for things they experience. For example, it can be quite confusing to children when one parent says, "I don't know why your mother doesn't call you when you're here. She probably doesn't care much about you," and the other parent says, "I called you three times last night. Why didn't you call back? Doesn't your dad give you the messages?" The child may not know which parent to believe. Parents need to understand how children feel when parents belittle each other or when the children are placed in confusing situations. Such experiences are never healthy for children and cause children to become confused, withdrawn, anxious, insecure, or polarized.

Parenting plans for children of this age group need the following:

• A structured and consistent time share that guarantees access to each parent, in ways that are appropriate. The best parenting plans range from a split of thirty-five percent to sixty-five percent of time with either parent (and thus a primary home), to relatively equal, 50-50 joint physical custody, in which the child is with each parent about half of the time. If your child had a strong relationship with you prior to your divorce, she may feel rejected by you if she doesn't see you enough after the divorce. While children often express a wish for equal time with both of their parents, this may either be to keep things fair or because they truly want to spend equal time with each of you. As you develop your own parenting plan, try to understand your child's true feelings, including what's behind her desire for equal time and what will work best in your family situation.

• While joint physical custody may be best in a given situation, it requires consistency and willingness to resolve your differences away from your child. It requires you to live near enough to one another so that your child does not spend lengthy amounts of time traveling between home, school, and friends. It also requires you to share all of the tasks of parenting and help your child and each other transfer your child's things (school supplies, athletic equipment, etc.) from one house to the other without conflict.

• Your time-share needs to promote your strengths, while giving each of you time alone to recover from the divorce.

• Exchanges should minimize your child's exposure to conflict. School or other neutral places are excellent transition places between Mom's house and Dad's house.

• You must find ways to keep your children out of the middle of your conflicts. Do not have your child deliver messages to the other parent, or ask your child to tell you what the other parent is doing. Avoid having your child spy on the other parent or be forced into talking about what goes on in the other parent's home. Communication needs to be between parents only, even if this requires help from a neutral professional. More on that in chapter 9.

• To the extent you can, there should be a plan for co-parenting. If your conflict is more extreme, a pattern of parallel parenting and avoidance of each other is best (refer to the discussion of cooperative vs. parallel parenting styles in chapter 2).

Adolescents (13–17 years)

The major task of the adolescent is developing greater independence and separation from the family. Some adolescents are oppositional and negative, though many are easy-going and delightful. Just as with the toddler, the primary task during adolescence is identify formation, which can lead to challenges due to resistance and rebelliousness. Healthy adolescents function well in school, have self-confidence, and positive peer relationships. They talk with their parents about life goals, and they begin to plan for driving and dating, as well as college and careers. As a group, adolescents are at risk of being moody. At times, they may feel overwhelmed by pressure from many sources, including friends, negative peer influences, and pressures at school. They may use poor judgment and feel insecure. Their ideas, values, and goals may change considerably over the course of junior and senior high school. However, these years can be exciting ones as your teen grows into a productive and idealistic young adult.

Constant adjustment and conflict puts this population at potential risk for academic failure, eating and sleeping disorders, depression, suicide, delinquency, promiscuity, or substance abuse. To make matters worse, adolescents tend to withdraw and isolate themselves from parents, so the signs of these symptoms may not be obvious.

When a divorce occurs at this age, teens worry about the loss of their family life. They tend to feel responsible, guilty, and angry for the way the divorce affects them. Children of this age tend to be somewhat naturally self-centered, and divorce is a disruption in their lives. Many teens avoid *both* parents after a separation, especially if the parents burden them with loyalty conflicts and adult problems.

Some adolescents isolate themselves to their room and want little or nothing to do with one of their parents. This may be the result of alienation by one parent. Sometimes it is the result of frustration with the conflict; sometimes it relates to the moral outrage felt toward one parent's behavior; sometimes it is the result of legitimate frustration that has built up over a long, painful relationship. When an older adolescent (15–17) is adamant about how he wants the parenting plan to be, it is important for parents to listen to him (unless, of course, it is unhealthy or unsafe). Parents do not want to set up a situation that may encourage an adolescent to rebel (any more than adolescents do normally!).

Parenting plans for children of this age group should include the following considerations:

• A time share plan which incorporates a range of possibilities. Many adolescents prefer one primary home (in large part to avoid confusion for their friends), and weekends or evenings with the other parent. Some will prefer a balanced, fifty-fifty plan with their parents. Much of this will depend on the history of the relationships with each of you and your availability to meet their adolescent-related needs. At times, adolescents may use one parent's home to get a break from the other parent or from their siblings. More than anything, your adolescent will usually want a say in your parenting plan.

• If you have more than one child you may need a different schedule for each child. If that is the case, you may want a schedule that allows all of your children to be together at certain times.

• You need to manage your conflicts away from your teen and maintain healthy limits with them. Confiding in adult issues with your teen only increases her risk of feeling overwhelmed by your divorce.

• Parenting at this age is often like being a good mentor. Parents need to have rules and structure but allow their child the freedom to explore and grow as they form their growing identity. Work to listen to your child and understand her ideas, ideals, and angst. At times, you will feel like a chauffer, frequently taking your child to her activities. While you may want a more relaxed life with your children, parenting an adolescent can involve all of this.

• In cases of severe high-conflict, your teen will probably detach from both of you. She may need other appropriate supportive adults. In such cases a therapist, friend's parent, or school counselor may need to monitor and assess risks.

Reassure Your Child, Regardless of Age

No matter your children's ages, they need reassurance to know they are loved by, and are free to love, both parents. Very young children need lots of tender loving care, hugs, and special time. This can include time set aside to talk about feelings and to read to your child. Bedtime routines that incorporate soothing and nurturing are particularly helpful.

School-age children also need reassurance, which can be expressed by supporting their interests, encouraging their friendships, and understanding their feelings. Children of this age need parents to actively support their love of — and relationship with — the other parent. These children are especially vulnerable to conflict, and need parents to communicate with each other. Do not use your children as messengers or spies!

Finally, adolescents find reassurance when parents support their growing independence. Rules and routines are critical for this age group. You will need to be available for open and honest discussions about everything life has to offer.

At every age, listen to your child's feelings, make and follow rules you believe in, nurture your child's self-esteem, and support your child's relationship with the other parent. Parents can be an excellent example of conflict-resolution. Teach them the skills they will need to be independent adults, while encouraging them to understand themselves and make goals for the future.

Things to Remember

• Divorce affects children differently, depending on their ages and stage of development.

• It's important to provide as much stability as possible for toddlers and very young children.

• Structure and routine are key elements of a stable home environment for school-age children.

• Teens, struggling with their own independence, may attempt to distance themselves from both parents during a divorce, especially one that is full of conflict.

• Children of all ages need support, love and reassurance. It is very important that they know that the divorce is something that happened between their parents; they did not cause it.

CHAPTER 5

Talking to Your Children

"Our lives are not determined by what happens to us, but how we react to what happens; not by what life brings to us, but by the attitude we bring to life. A positive attitude causes a chain reaction of positive thoughts, events, and outcomes. It is a catalyst . . . a spark that creates extraordinary results."

— Anonymous

Like so many parents, Bob and Alice Johnson have been arguing for years. Their children have been aware of the conflicts, and have been concerned that they might get a divorce. As their conflicts worsened, they decided to go ahead with the divorce. Their primary concern, at least at the beginning, was how to talk about the divorce with their children. Both of them have tried unsuccessfully to shield the children from the conflicts. They are worried about telling their children too much about the conflicts, and don't want to upset their children by saying the wrong thing. They can't agree on custody and visitation, who's going to stay in the family home, if the home will need to be sold, or how to talk to their children about these uncertainties. They want to handle their divorce in a way that is least damaging to their children.

BECAUSE THE JOHNSONS ARE SO WORRIED about what to tell the children, they haven't told them anything. The children are worried about their parents and sense the pending separation. They ask their parents questions, but, because they don't know what to say, both parents avoid direct responses; it becomes the dreaded "D" word. Because their questions go unanswered, the children become anxious and insecure.

❖　❖　❖　❖　❖

David and Amber Smith have argued in front of their children for years. Like some parents, they seem to have little ability to argue behind closed doors, and since their separation, both parents have included the children in all of their disputes. They tell their children everything, often confusing them with different stories.

The children learned from Dad that Mother's boyfriend caused the breakup of the marriage. They learned from their mother that Dad has been emotionally abusive. Both parents tell the children about the finances, and encourage them to participate in the custody dispute. The children are tired of it and don't want to be told anything.

❖ ❖ ❖ ❖ ❖

As these two examples illustrate, parents need to be careful about what to tell their children and how they do it. It is easy to make mistakes in both directions, either telling children too little or telling them too much. Research over the past several years suggests that the majority of parents going through a divorce do not tell their children enough about the many changes that will be happening in their life. Other parents, embroiled in high conflict, tell their children too much about what has been going on, often blaming the other parent in the process. This chapter focuses on talking to your children about divorce-related issues, while continuing to maintain healthy boundaries in what you say to them, and answering their questions in a thoughtful and reasonable way. You might be able to do some of this in your own home, perhaps in a family discussion or in the privacy of your child's bedroom. Other discussions may be more difficult and perhaps can best be accomplished in a therapist's office. As a general rule of thumb, normal day-to-day discussions should be easiest between a parent and a child and flow naturally from the child's questions. However, tougher, more problematic circumstances may require the assistance of a therapist.

Four Basic Principles

In talking with your children, there are four major principles that you'll want to consider. First, you'll want to *think about your child's statements and questions* and *answer them directly and honestly*, without any derogatory comments about the other parent. For example, if your child tells you, "Mom says you're mean sometimes," you'll want to respond with something like, "I'm glad you brought this up. It's OK if Mom thinks I'm mean sometimes, but what's important is what you and I think. You'll probably feel that I'm mean when I make you clean your room and send you to bed at a certain time. I sometimes get mad and yell, and when I do, I'm probably acting mean. What do you think?" You wouldn't want to say something like, "Well, Mom can be real mean too. She's always yelling. That's why I divorced her, because of her meanness."

A second principle is to *pay attention to your child's feelings*, especially the ones that aren't being expressed. If you're paying more attention to the feelings than the facts, you'll respond to the same question with something like, "What are you feeling when you hear that? Have you talked with your mom about those feelings? Do you sometimes think I'm mean? I guess we all get mean sometimes. You and I need to talk about it when you think I'm being mean." By acknowledging your child's feelings, you are not judging her or her feelings, but helping her understand them. Again, you want to avoid criticizing the other parent.

The third consideration is to *try to read between the lines* of your child's statements and questions. Often there's some hidden concern that your child is reluctant to mention. Your response might address that, as well. "I bet it's hard for you when your mom and I say things like that. You know, if you think I'm being mean, or if you have a hard time with our divorce, it's something we need to talk about. I hope you can feel free to come to me with anything that concerns you." With this type of response, you're acknowledging the feelings, and suggesting that there could be more to your child's statement than just what's on the surface.

The final principle is helping your child *define concepts* in his life. Young children are very concrete and don't understand abstract concepts like relationships. Even at a basic level, they may not understand the difference between a mom and a step-mom. They may not understand their various feelings. Children under age five don't fully understand time concepts and may not be able to comprehend the concept of "in a couple of days," or "next week." Older children need to learn about more abstract concepts of life, such as how to resolve conflicts and differences in relationships, thinking about goals and interests, and planning for their future. You'll want to consider these things when talking with your child.

The rest of this chapter will focus on discussing the divorce with your child — initially and over time. I'll present some typical questions and comments that children make at different ages. Using the principles above, I'll provide sample responses to help you answer questions directly, consider your child's feelings, read between the lines, and explain concepts.

Telling Your Child About Your Divorce

Once you've made the decision to get a divorce, your first task is to make a plan for talking to your children about the divorce. This is not something to do impulsively! Instead, talk with the other parent about what you know is happening and how you would like to tell your children. Some things may be known, such as who will be moving out, when that is happening, and where each of you is going to be living. You may not know all the details, or you might not have a custody and visitation plan set, but by recognizing the differences between short-term and long-term plans, and understanding the things that you do know, you can develop a plan for talking to your children.

It is important for both of you to talk with one another about how you will tell your children about your divorce before you tell them. This is the first step in helping them recognize that you will work together on their behalf. Reach an agreement about what to tell your children, and be aware that each of you might want to emphasize different things. Once you have this agreement in place, it's important to agree to share the news with your children together in a family environment, and be certain that everyone has a chance to talk and express feelings.

At this initial meeting, tell your children the following:

- That you're getting separated or divorced, with a very brief discussion of the reasons (e.g., that you are tired of fighting, that you can no longer live together, or whatever the basic reason is).

- That you both still love them, and that they had nothing to do with your decision to separate.

- That you will both continue to love them even though the marriage is coming to an end.

- That you both will stay involved in their lives and participate as you have in the past.

- That you've both worked hard to try to stay together, but that isn't going to happen.

- That you're sad abut the breakup, and you expect that they too are likely to feel sad at first, and that you will all work together to feel better.

- That, while it is hard to understand now, you expect that everyone in the family will feel better over the next year or two.

Those are the initial basics that everyone should tell their children when planning to separate. *Stop and listen to your children.* They are likely to be crying. Comfort them and help them with those feelings. Let them ask questions and try to answer their questions honestly and carefully. Avoid blame, and be clear that this is a mutual decision based on mutual problems in the relationship. Encourage them to ask questions then — and at any time in the future — about the separation, express their feelings, and to share what this is like for them.

Don't go into details about adult issues or talk about your sexual relationship, money, or emotional or physical abuse. Those subjects tend to generate blame and are not appropriate for children. There may become a time when those issues are relevant, especially if your children bring them up as they get older, but the initial discussion about your separation is not the time to raise them. Be sensitive to the fact that your separation will be a shock to your children, and avoid telling them too much.

Help your children understand that there is a difference between short-term and long-term issues. Tell them what you know about the initial logistics, including who is moving out, what the initial access arrangements will be, and what the initial temporary plans are. If your intent is to share custody, reassure your children that you will both be active in their lives and see them on a regular basis, even though there will be some adjustments and changes in their lives. Try to have at least a temporary parenting plan in place when you tell the children so that you can share with them the details of that plan. Constantly remind them that you both love them and reassure them that you both will be there for them. Children are likely to keep their insecurities and fears to themselves so it may not be apparent that they need this reassurance. While it's important for all parents to tell their children that they love them, children whose parents are going through divorce need double the reassurance, double the affection, and double the nurturing. The first meeting discussing the divorce is a great place to start this reassurance.

At the same time, it is likely that there will be many unanswerable questions. Be honest with them that you don't know everything *now*, but reassure them that you will work together to find answers to their questions *as soon as you have them.* Help them understand that your goal is to make everyone's life less painful, and reassure them that you will work toward this goal. Your children will adjust to your divorce best if the two of you work together to improve things and reduce conflict. In contrast, your children will have a difficult time adjusting to your divorce when your conflicts continue or intensify after your divorce. Reassure your children of your goal to reduce the overall conflict in their lives, and help them understand that you're getting your divorce to make everyone's life more peaceful. Reassure them that even though you have stopped loving the other parent, you will not stop loving them.

It is quite likely that, over the next few weeks, your children will have a wide range of emotions and responses. They may act as if nothing has changed and keep their feelings to themselves, or they may seem sad and cry a lot. They may ask either few or many questions. This is a difficult time because of your own emotions, but it is important to be sensitive to your children's feelings, encouraging them to talk and ask questions, while you continue to reassure them. At the beginning, it is important to find time every day to ask your children if they have any questions about what you've told them, and whether they have any feelings that they want to share. Your children's most common fears are related to the changes in their life and their most common question is "Why?" Avoid saying, "We're getting a divorce because your mother yells all the time." Instead, "We're getting a divorce because we can't stop fighting" is more helpful. In these first few weeks the primary focus should be on helping your children become accustomed to the idea of the separation, helping them settle into a potential new routine, and reassuring them that you will be there for them.

During the next few months, it is important to establish your new routines, settle into those routines, and continue to reassure your children frequently. Try to talk to your children about their feelings at least twice a week and ask if they have any questions. Ask them how they are feeling about your actions since the separation. When they ask questions pertaining to the other parent, answer them respectfully and fairly. Avoid criticizing the other parent while supporting and nurturing your child's feelings. For example, if your child comes home and tells you that the other parent has been "mean," consider that the child may be trying to pit one of you against the other. A response such as "Tell me about that," is a good first step, and after she has told you more, encourage her to talk with the other parent about her feelings. Then follow up with something like "I'm glad you could tell me about some of your concerns at Mom's house, and always feel free to tell me anything. I hope you'll also let me know if there are things that I'm doing that you don't like." This style enables your child to feel comforted by your neutrality and your willingness to talk about your own role in these issues.

After parents have been separated for some time, especially if they are in a routine that doesn't change, many parents forget to talk about divorce and those issues with their children. While it's not the daily topic that it might have been during the first few weeks of your separation, or the weekly topic during the first several months, it's still important to periodically talk with your child about the divorce and her feelings. It's very helpful for families to have a routine "family communication meeting," perhaps monthly, in which each person gets to bring up a topic to talk about. Even if questions aren't being asked, you might say to your child something like, "You know, your dad and I have been split up for about a year now, and we haven't talked about your feelings in a while. How's it going for you? What questions do you have?"

Many parents think that the only questions children have are the ones that they ask in the first month or two of separation. Remember that your child changes as she gets older, and may have new questions that she didn't even consider when you first separated. By periodically bringing up the issue, and encouraging your child's questions, you enable her to think about things in a different way and ask questions as they come up. In my work with children of divorce, I have found that most children keep their feelings to themselves unless parents encourage them and give them permission to talk and ask questions. Over time, this discussion may only come up three or four times per year, but it is still important to let your child know that you're available.

Remember to be neutral, acknowledge and focus on her feelings, give her lots of reassurance, and frequently tell your child that your love for her will not change. Demonstrate this with your words as well as your actions. Answer your child's questions truthfully, without blame or derogatory comments about the other parent, and at a level that is appropriate for her age. By following these guidelines, you'll be able to talk with your child on a regular and ongoing basis about your divorce and answer any questions she may have.

Specific Examples

While it is difficult to cover all of the examples that children might come up with, the following will demonstrate the principles described above. These examples are a guide to how you might consider responding to particular questions or statements that your child makes. Remember to be yourself and use your own words. Because children of various ages require different kinds of responses, examples are grouped according to age, and may be repeated for different ages. By studying these examples, and considering the kinds of questions your child typically asks, you can be prepared to help your child through the divorce process.

When Your Child is Four to Eight Years Old

With this age group, you'll want to answer questions simply and honestly. Try to introduce words for feelings and help your child understand the source of any anxiety or fears that she may have. Recognize that she won't understand things like an adult, so keep things simple and short. Avoid saying negative things about the other parent. Don't make excuses that aren't real, but at the same time, don't burden her with long explanations or with your emotions.

> *"Why don't you and Mommy love each other any more?"*
> "You know, honey, your mommy and I used to love each other. We tried hard, but we just can't live together any more. I bet you're scared that our love for you might change, but it won't. Your mommy or I might get mad at you, or you might even get mad at one of us, but we'll always love you and be here to take care of you."

In this response, you've focused on the fact that you tried, but things didn't work out, and you've addressed your child's fears and feelings. It's short, simple, and to the point.

> *"Why is Daddy so mean?"*
> "Sometimes your daddy gets angry, just like we all do. I know he still loves you. Have you tried to talk to him about what makes you upset? I'm sure he wants to know if you're feeling bad. You know, sometimes you'll think I'm being mean and if you do, I sure hope you'll tell me so that I can understand your feelings, too!"

In this response, you've tried to answer your child's question simply, without being critical of the other parent. You've addressed problem solving by asking if he's talked to his dad. You've also given permission for your child's feelings, and encouraged him to tell you if he thinks you're being mean.

> *"I miss Mommy. Why didn't she come to see me tonight"?*
> "I know it's been a few days since you saw your mom. You sure seem to feel sad, and I know you miss her. I'm sure everything is

all right, but I don't know what happened. She didn't call me, either. I'm sure she just couldn't make it. She'll let us know what happened and she'll see you soon. Why don't we call her and leave her a message? Then we can find out when she'll come to see you."

This response focuses on your child's feelings, helps to problem solve, reads between the lines by mentioning that things are all right with Mom, and helps in understanding the concept of time. If it isn't time for your child to be with her mom, show her on a calendar so she can see when Mom's coming. Use the calendar to help her count the days until the next time she will see the other parent.

> *"Mommy, sometimes I get scared when I'm trying to go to sleep."*
> "What are you scared of? Can we talk about it?" After she answers, you might add the following, "Things will be OK, honey. You know, there have been many changes in our life recently. Your dad and I have gotten divorced, and you've been sleeping in different beds. While I know you're scared, I also know that everything's going to be fine over the next few weeks. It just takes some time to feel right about things again."

Try to focus first on your child's feelings when he mentions them. Once you've done that, reassure him and help him understand there's a reason for feeling the way he does.

> *"How come you say that Johnny is my brother, but dad says he's my stepbrother?"*
> "I bet it's confusing to you when your dad and I tell you different things. I'm glad you came to ask me. When parents get divorced, sometimes we meet new people. If we marry someone else, we call that person a stepparent. A stepparent is someone who we come to love that acts like a parent, but isn't really your parent. Your dad will always be your only dad, but now that I've remarried, Ben is your stepdad and in our house, Ben will *act* like a dad. I'll always be your only mom, but if Dad gets remarried, his new wife will be your stepmom. In the same way, Johnny isn't your real brother, he is a step-brother. But in our family, Johnny certainly acts like your brother, and that's what we call him.

This response acknowledges the confusion and feelings that occur when parents say different things. It then explains the concept in concrete, age-appropriate terms.

When Your Child is Nine to Twelve Years Old

With this age, pay attention to the fact that your child may try to take care of you and your feelings. He'll also want things to be fair between the two of you. Make sure that you let your child express himself. He's becoming more abstract in the way he thinks, but you might still need to keep your explanations simple. Try and help your child understand that everyone has good and bad traits, and that part of life is learning to live with them. Most importantly, be sensitive to your child's feelings, and admit if you make mistakes or hurt your child's feelings. Continue to avoid being critical of the other parent.

> *"Why did you and Dad get divorced?"*
> "You know, honey, sometimes adults just can't get along. We tried everything we could to stop our fighting. Your dad's a good person, and so am I, but we found out we're just not able to stay married. But, you know, we both love you and we'll always love you. That'll never change. And I know you love both of us, and that won't change, either. I know that right now you feel sad about this, and so do I. But keep in mind that we're *all* better off if your dad and I are happier. I know that in the long run we'll be happier living apart, even if it's hard to see it now."

In this response, you're pointing out the facts, acknowledging a balanced view of relationships, and reassuring your child. You're also acknowledging your child's feelings, and yours.

> *"Why does Mom yell so much?"*
> "I wonder what you're feeling when she yells. What do you do with those feelings? Is that something you'd like Mom to know? Let's talk about ways you could talk to Mom."

This might help you sort out and understand your child's feelings and reassure her that you're listening. If you want to give more of an explanation about stress and anger, and how people deal with their feelings and relationships differently, you might also say something like the following:

> "Honey, sometimes we all get stressed out. One of the ways Mom deals with it is to yell. When I get stressed, you might not see it as much. I stay at work or exercise to help me when I get stressed. Keep in mind that even if your mom yells, she still loves you. When she's in a better mood, try to let her know it bothers you when she yells. You know, sometimes your friend Jamie is kind of mean, but you always work it out and keep playing with

her. Sometimes you're a little bossy, and you and I work it out. You and Mom can do the same. Don't forget to let me know if I do things that bother you. That way, you and I can work on making our relationship better, too."

"Why do you always ask me about Mom?"
"I'm sorry, honey, I didn't know it bothered you! I wanted to make sure you were happy with things, and I was wrong. I'll try to stop asking about her. I certainly don't want you to feel like you have to protect either of us or our feelings. If you want to talk about things at Mom's, that's fine, but I'll try not to ask about her anymore if it bothers you."

This is a perfect opportunity to explain that you make mistakes and you're sorry when you do. You help by explaining your intentions, and then honor your child's feelings by saying that you won't ask about things in a way that bothers her.

"How come I can't take my Game-Boy over to Dad's?"
"Honey, I'm sorry that you think I won't let you take it. You're right, it's yours, and you should be able to take it if you want. However, it was pretty expensive, so remember to bring it back, or else you won't have it here when you want it here. As far as I'm concerned, you can take your things to anyone's house you want, just remember to keep track of them and bring them home."

Again, this is a good opportunity to apologize to your child and work things out. Especially with the older children in this age group, you'll want to try to resolve your differences and try to see things from their perspective.

"Mom lets me stay up till 10:00. How come you make me go to bed at 9:00?"
"Sometimes when I hear you compare the differences between Mom's house and mine, I wonder if you're upset about our divorce and having to go back and forth. Is that hard for you? Let your mom and me know what it's like so that we can make it easier.

"On the other hand, I bet it's confusing to you when mom and I have different rules. There's nothing wrong with her rules and nothing wrong with mine. We just do things differently. We both want you to get enough sleep. I'll talk with your mom and see if we can get a little closer in some of our rules, but in the meantime, when you're here, you and I need to work things out. Perhaps you can stay up until 9:30, as long as you get up with no problems in the morning. But I want you to use that extra half-hour to read or do something quiet, rather than just watching TV or tearing around."

In this example, you're reading between the lines, wondering if his question has more to do with the divorce and the moving back and forth between homes than it does with the rules. You're also explaining in a neutral way that there are lots of different types of rules, and that neither is wrong or right. You're acknowledging the confusing feelings, and you're helping to resolve things. Keep it up!

When Your Child is Thirteen or Older

With this age group, you'll want to consider the long-term teaching that you do. Adolescents can certainly handle more abstract issues about relationships and what makes them work and why they can be troublesome. They're very concerned with their daily life and their future. Many of these children need direction and an opportunity to think about things. They can certainly learn that things don't always get settled in one conversation, and that you may need to come back to the discussion at a later time. Finally, because children in this age group can be so self-centered and so focused on separation issues, it's important to help them maintain a perspective beyond their current feelings.

> *"Why do I have to go over to Dad's? I don't like him."*
> "I think we need to talk about all of your feelings. What's the problem at Dad's? Can you talk with him about any of this? You know, lots of times we don't like some things about someone, but then we find a way to work it out. Relationships aren't always easy, even with people we're close to. Perhaps you and Dad can learn to talk together like you and I can. Do you think some counseling would help you with these feelings? I also wonder if you and Dad have talked about the amount of time that you go there. You might find a way to compromise this with him."

Clearly, you wouldn't say all of this at one time. However, each of these responses conveys that you care, that you understand his feelings, that there are ways to resolve his differences with his father, and that relationships take work. This is good guidance for your teen.

> *"How do I know if my girlfriend's just using me?"*
> "Boy, you sound scared. It takes time to build trust in a new relationship. It might have been easier if Mom and I hadn't gotten divorced; sometimes divorce makes kids nervous in their own relationships. Relationships can be lots of work, and they change over time. That's part of why it didn't work out with your mom

and me. But you and I have always worked things out, even when one of us was angry or hurt. Perhaps you can apply that same feeling to your relationship with your girlfriend. Talk with her, get to know her, and let her know you and your feelings. Trust grows over time, and as long as you keep working at it, you'll learn what you like and don't like about each other. Use that as a way to figure out what you need in a relationship, and what she might need. As you keep doing this, you'll find that it feels right, or it doesn't. If it does, keep building on that. If not, you'll need to learn to compromise and work things out, or learn how to decide the relationship isn't right anymore. You might not know right away, but we'll keep talking about it while you try and figure it out."

Again, you might not say all of this at once, but you certainly want to convey that the reason he's fearful and that trust is hard to establish is because of the fact that he's seen you get divorced. You're also talking about how to communicate in a relationship, and how to point out that different people have different needs. It's good to end this by encouraging your child to come back to the conversation at a later date, as he learns more about the relationship and his own feelings and needs.

"Why do I have to go to Mom's just because Janie (his sister) is going?"
"You never did like having to do things just because of Janie. Perhaps you and Mom and I can talk about your schedule and when you see each of us. I don't know that you *have* to keep the same schedule, though there are times that you and Mom and Janie should all be together, just like there are times that you and Janie and I should all be together. Let's see what Mom says and we'll find a solution."

One of the biggest issues for adolescents is the way in which they're often grouped together with their siblings. This can become a burden for them. Because their needs are so different than their younger brothers and sisters, and because they often become vocal about it, it's something that has to be addressed. Be prepared to treat your teenage child different than his younger siblings, and talk with him like the young adult he's becoming.

"Mom, I just hate it when Dad yells at all of us. What can we do?"

This is an opportunity to talk more about feelings and the options in your child's life. Help your child understand what causes

Dad to yell and how to deal with it. Explain to her that she may want to hold on to certain relationships — even with people who don't treat her very well — because they're important people in her life, that she doesn't have to put up with people who treat her poorly if they're *not* important in her life. Most importantly, teach her to discriminate between what she wants to accept in her life and what she doesn't.

> "I know you don't like it when people yell; you never have. Have you tried to talk with him about it? I know Dad doesn't want to hurt you, even though he does yell when he gets stressed. Try to talk with him alone when you get the chance so that you can feel better. It's really important that you are respected in any relationship, and I'm sure your dad respects you. He just needs to work with you to express it better."

At another point in time, you might say:

> "If you're in a relationship with someone who treats you in a way you don't like, you might try to work it out. If it's someone important to you, like your dad, you'll want to strengthen the relationship and heal those feelings. If it's someone like a new boyfriend, you can end the relationship if it isn't working out for you. *Never* stay in a relationship that you believe to be abusive to you."

Things to Remember

• Answer your child(ren)'s questions about the divorce directly and honestly.

• Pay attention to your child(ren)'s feelings. Try to read between the lines of your child's statements and questions about the divorce.

• Tell your children about the divorce in a way that is appropriate to their age levels.

• Continue talking with your children about the divorce, even after things have settled into a routine.

• Reassure your children that mommy and daddy both still love them, and the divorce is not their fault.

• Help your children to understand some of the ways that life will be different now, while reassuring them that your love for them will not change. For instance, there may be different rules at mommy's and daddy's houses, but both of you will remain actively involved in their life.

CHAPTER 6

Children Aren't Property

It's Your Child's Life

"People spend a lifetime searching for happiness; looking for peace. They chase idle dreams, addictions, religions, even other people, hoping to fill the emptiness that plagues them. The irony is the only place they ever needed to search was within."
— Ramona L. Anderson

Janelle, 12, is a girl scout who enjoys participating in weekly meetings and monthly camping activities. However, at the beginning of each year, she is forced to miss the first week or two because her parents can't agree on who is going to fill out the paperwork. They argue about whose responsibility it is, and whether or not Janelle should take responsibility for this task. Also, since Janelle's dad only sees her three out of five weekends, she has to miss several camping trips per year because he is unwilling to give up his time for Janelle's scouting trips. While stating that he supports her scouting, he is very clear that he will only allow Janelle to go on these trips if Janelle's mother will trade weekends so that he doesn't lose his time. Mother, however, is reluctant to trade weekends because she feels that Father should simply allow Janelle to go on her camping trips regardless of whose weekend it is. None of these problems existed before Janelle's parents were divorced when she was 10, as both parents supported and encouraged her participation in all of her scouting activities. Unfortunately, Janelle has decided that she's going to give up scouting because "it's no longer any fun."

❖　❖　❖　❖　❖

THIS EXAMPLE SHOWS how some children are hurt after parents get divorced. Most parents raise their children with certain goals in mind. These often include the desire to participate in chosen activities, help them with school, encourage them to be productive, and spend time with friends. You want to teach your child and guide her as she makes her choices in the world.

Just as you buy your child her clothes, feed her, and share your values and possessions with her, you encourage her abilities, interests, and activities in a healthy and positive way. It is in these ways that you show your child that you value her health and education and want her to grow into a productive adult with healthy social values and good self-esteem.

❖   ❖   ❖   ❖   ❖

Kyle, age 12, has none of Janelle's difficulties. While his parents rarely speak to each other by phone, and do nearly all of their communication either by written correspondence or in a mediator's office, Kyle has not missed a scouting event in three years. Like Janelle, Kyle only spends a moderate amount of weekend time with his father, but his father willingly gives up his time so that Kyle can participate in his chosen activity. Each year when it is time to fill out the paperwork, Mother is sure to pass the paperwork to Father who adds his information and sends the paperwork back to Mother. Kyle needn't worry about being a messenger. When it is possible, both of Kyle's parents participate in camping trips, according to Kyle's wishes and regardless of whose "weekend time" it is. Not surprisingly, Kyle continues to find scouting fun and is pleased with his accomplishments.

❖   ❖   ❖   ❖   ❖

It is clear that Kyle's parents, in spite of their vast differences and inability to communicate about nearly everything, are able to put aside their differences enough to allow Kyle to participate in his desired activity. Because they are able to keep him out of the middle and cooperate enough to get the necessary paperwork completed, he is not overwhelmed by their conflict. Since they don't argue about the money or the time, he is able to feel proud of his participation and accomplishments. Janelle's parents, in contrast, are unable to set aside their differences. Instead of enjoying her activity and feeling the support and encouragement of her parents, Janelle feels bad, misses many of the activities, and becomes withdrawn. While it's understandable that your child might have to miss a scouting event because of a significant family trip, or be told that he can't take his video games to a friend's house because they are very expensive, it is not understandable for your child to miss an important activity or special opportunity because one of you is unwilling to give up your "time." Treat your child with respect and encourage her participation in activities regardless of your desires and needs.

Divorce is a process which has the potential to destroy the hopes and dreams of many parents. When the family unit is broken, many parents want to hang on to everything they can. Some parents cling to their children and interfere with their development. Other parents fight over possessions, especially those that have been given to the children by the parents. Whereas parents once encouraged the child's participation in activities such as soccer or music, many now become more concerned with "my weekend," and are reluctant to share in their child's activities. With the added financial burdens caused by divorce, many parents have to work more and have less time to spend with their children.

With these changes, many parents become frustrated and angry. However, when parents become frustrated and angry at each other, the education and self-esteem of their children is at risk. When parents get caught up in battles with each other, they no longer have time to help children with homework or participate in their special activities. Worse yet, some parents spend all of their resources on the divorce and custody litigation, leaving little or no money for college. Surely it is the children who suffer in these circumstances.

However, divorce doesn't have to destroy your dreams for your child or his wishes. Both of you can stay involved and supportive of your children, regardless of whether or not you like each other. You simply have to swallow your pride and do what it takes for your child. This chapter will focus on how you can preserve your child's activities and interests, and regain the values that you may have lost as a result of your divorce.

Your Child's Activities, School Life and Social Life

Your main task is to place more emphasis on supporting your child's interests and activities than you do on hating your ex-spouse. If you encouraged your child's participation in sports before your divorce, you need to continue supporting her participation after your divorce. Your primary parenting job after your divorce is to help your child adjust. She needs stability and consistency. Don't force her to make unnecessary changes in her life. Remember that her activities are a source of emotional support and self-esteem for her. If your daughter played soccer before you divorced, her friends and coaches will be an important part of her support system. If you begin to argue about her participation in soccer, she will feel bad, and may begin to blame herself for your conflicts, even though there is no reason for her to feel that way. She may start to feel that you hate each other more than you love her.

If you encouraged your teen-aged child to baby-sit or work part-time before you separated, you shouldn't object to him baby-sitting or working just because he wants to do it on "your weekend." As your child moves into adolescence, he needs to begin feeling more independent. He can't do this very well if you start arguing about whether he's going to work on "your time" or the other parent's time.

Some parents live a bit farther away from their child and don't feel too comfortable in the other parent's community. However, your child will want you to become involved in his life. Get to know your son's friends and his interests. Take him to birthday parties that fall on your weekend, even if they're in the other parent's community. Regardless of where his friends live, they are *his* friends and you need to support those relationships. Even though it may be hard, you need to continue supporting your child's social life, school work, and extra-curricular activities just as you did before your divorce. Your child will be pleased — and adjust in a healthier way to your divorce — if you do.

As your child gets older, it is common to find that you are giving up your time for her activities more frequently than when she was younger. This is true for all parents, not just divorced ones, though many divorced parents feel that this is magnified since they spend limited time with their child due to the changes following the divorce. Rather than getting upset and arguing with your child, however, recognize that it is healthy for her to get involved in several activities and have many outside interests as they grow up. Remember, even if you *hadn't* gotten a divorce, your adolescent child would be spending less time with you than she did when she was younger. As mentioned in chapter 4, this is a normal part of her development. Don't take it personally and expect her to stay home with you when she would rather be starting to work or be with her friends. Continue to support her interests just as you would have if you weren't divorced.

Your Child's Toys and Clothes

Kevin, age 4, lives with his mother during the week and spends weekends with his father. For his recent birthday, his father bought him a special teddy bear, and his mother got him a new bicycle with training wheels. Like most children, Kevin wants to be able to use these toys whenever he chooses. However, because his parents are constantly arguing over clothing, time, and activities, neither Kevin's mother nor his father is willing to let Kevin take his toys over to the other parent's house. Kevin is forced to live a life in which his cherished bicycle and favorite stuffed animal are left behind each and every time he changes households. Kevin feels sad and is forced to re-experience the difficulty of separation and divorce each time he makes a transition between homes. Since Kevin can't control his things, he begins to act controlling and bossy to others.

When a child has a special object that provides comfort wherever he is, it is said to be a "transitional object." Transitional objects are very important to young children, especially when they are feeling insecure. Allowing your child to take her cherished transitional objects to the other parent's house helps your child adjust to difficult things in his life, including your divorce.

> Caitlin's parents, in contrast to Kevin's, allow her to take her things from one home to the other. When she gets a special sweatshirt from Mom, it can go to Dad's house and Mom doesn't mind, even if she accidentally leaves it there. Similarly, when Dad buys Caitlin a stuffed animal, he knows that Caitlin wants to take it back and forth between houses. Her parents don't feel possessive about the items they buy for Caitlin and she is allowed to control her own belongings and use them as she sees fit. Caitlin's parents are encouraging her to share with her younger brother, Sam. As a result of Caitlin observing her parents' ability to share with each other, it's easier for her to share her own toys and things with her little brother.

When you allow your child to carry toys and belongings to the other parent's home, the worst that can happen is that a toy gets broken or an item gets lost. When you don't allow him to share his toys and things with the other parent, your child's *feelings* get broken and his *spirit* gets lost. Your child needs to be able to share his things between both homes, regardless of your time share.

In these examples, Kevin's and Caitlin's feelings, self-esteem and behaviors are affected by the ability of parents to allow them to have their *own* lives, activities, and possessions, rather than competing with each other about these items. Time and again, I see children who have lost their spirit and are feeling confused, sad, and anxious because their parents have different expectations after the divorce.

Rather than keeping score about who buys what, if you buy your child nice clothes and rarely see them again because the other parent keeps them at her house, enjoy the fact that your daughter has nice clothes much of the time, whether she is with you or not. If you buy her a new teddy bear and she wants to keep it at her dad's, understand that this might help her feel closer to *you* when she is away. Learn to understand your child's behavior and what it means to her. At the same time, if the other parent lets your son bring his expensive video game over to your house, encourage your son to take care of it and make sure that he takes it back to dad's so that he can use it there as well.

Separating Your Life from Your Child's

It is important for you to separate your own wishes, feelings, and needs from those of your child. This is true for all parents, but even more important if you are divorced. Kyle's dad is able to separate his need for time with Kyle, allowing Kyle to be at his scouting weekends. Caitlin's mom is able to separate her competitive feelings toward Caitlin's dad from the need for Caitlin to have her bike wherever she wants it. Parents who save their financial resources to provide a college fund for their children are able to separate their desire to win litigation now from their child's need for a college education later. The two key ingredients here are empathy and the ability to put your child's needs first.

Empathy is a process in which you put yourself in another person's place and try to understand his or her feelings. Having empathy for your child is an important task of parenting, as it enables you to understand your child's experiences and feelings, and act in a way to help your child feel better. In the example above, Caitlin's parents have empathy for her anxiety and encourage her to take items of importance between houses in order to reduce her anxiety. In contrast, Kevin's parents have little empathy for his anxiety, putting him in a position where he feels more anxious and upset. Kevin's situation is made even worse when his parents punish him for his controlling behavior and stubbornness, without recognizing that his insecurity is a prime cause of his behavior. If Kevin's parents had empathy for him, they would understand his anxiety and attempt to help him reduce it. They would also understand their own role in contributing to his anxiety by their competitive actions.

One way to develop empathy is to learn to understand both your child's behavior and her emotions. Parents tend to focus more on their child's behavior, rather than her emotions, because it's easier to see behaviors than connect to hidden emotions. It's not hard to recognize when your child is bossy, but it may be more difficult to see when your child is afraid. Many children keep their feelings to themselves, and many children aren't aware of what their feelings mean. When you see your child acting in a way you don't approve of, set limits on her behavior, but also try to understand her feelings.

For example, when your child is bossy toward you, you might say to her, "it's not polite to boss others around. I won't be treated that way." Follow up by saying, "You know, sometimes when children act bossy, they feel bossed by others. Have I done anything to make you feel bossed around? Is anything bothering you that you haven't talked about?" These statements give her the message that you won't accept her bossy behavior, but also that she should think about why she is acting that way. It's important for parents to think about the connection between their children's behavior and feelings, and to teach their children to recognize it as well.

As you work on developing empathy for your child, you will also want to learn how to put your child's needs first. Determine how difficult you want things to be. If you fight with your ex and ignore your child's feelings, she will have problems. If you have empathy for her feelings and put her needs first, she will feel loved and learn that even though her parents have divorced, her life doesn't have to change very much. Janelle's parents had little empathy for her feelings, and therefore had difficulty putting her need to participate in scouts above their need to compete with one another. In contrast, Kyle's parents do a good job of recognizing how important his activities are, putting his needs first, and finding a different way to deal with their own feelings, wishes, and desires.

Effective parents:

- separate their own needs from the needs of their children
- show empathy for their children and their children's feelings
- put their children's needs first
- allow their children to participate in activities chosen by the children, regardless of custody and visitation issues
- allow their children freely to take toys, clothes, and "transition objects" (such as teddy bears) between each parent's home.

Setting Up Healthy Boundaries

Ultimately, if you want to honor your children's needs, activities, and possessions, you will need to set up healthy boundaries between yourself and your child. The first step in setting up healthy boundaries is to *understand* your own feelings. As you do this, you will also better learn to understand your motives and behaviors, and how your emotions affect your behaviors. These are critical first steps in developing empathy and setting up boundaries between you and your child.

As described above, Kevin's parents do not seem to understand their level of competition with each other, so they certainly can't understand how their competition is preventing them from letting Kevin take his things between houses. In contrast, Kyle's dad understands his own desire for more time with Kyle. He knows that he misses Kyle when Kyle is with his mother and at his activities. However, he also knows how important Kyle's activities are, and he has the ability to differentiate between *his* needs and *Kyle's* needs. He has healthy boundaries between his feelings and Kyle's, so he lets Kyle do what he wants in spite of his own sense of loss.

The second step in setting up healthy boundaries is to *separate* your own feelings and needs from those of your child. Kyle's dad understands his needs and feelings, and then separates these needs and feelings from his actions toward Kyle. All too often, parents confuse their feelings with their children's and use the confusion to justify their selfish behavior. Janelle's dad doesn't let her go to scouting events on his weekends, and states, "Janelle needs to be with me for all of our scheduled time." Unfortunately, this is not Janelle's need, but a manifestation of Dad's need to have Janelle with him. If Janelle's father understood his own need, and separated it from Janelle's need, and if he had empathy for Janelle's desire and need to participate in her chosen and desired activities, Janelle would be able to go to her scouting events regardless of when they were scheduled. Developing an ability to separate your own thoughts, feelings, and needs from those of your children is a critical second step in setting up healthy boundaries.

It will be easier if you remember that you do not own your child's time. Judges, attorneys, and mental health professionals hear parents talk about "my time" with the children. It's not *your* time, but rather your *child's* time. Time is not property that you own. Your child has a life, full of *his* chosen activities. As parents, it's your responsibility to nurture your child and ensure that he participates in these chosen activities. Maintain the attitude that it is your child's time, shared with you according to the parenting plan, and you will more easily maintain healthy boundaries.

The third step in maintaining healthy boundaries with your child is to *open the lines of communication*. Once you understand your own feelings, and can separate them from your child's feelings, you need to understand what his thoughts and feelings really are. While empathy will help you get some understanding of his feelings, keeping the lines of communication open is essential. One of the reasons Kyle is able to participate as fully as he does in his scouting activities is that he tells both parents how important it is to him. In contrast, Janelle, as a result of being inappropriately drawn into her parent's conflicts, is afraid to tell her father *her* true feelings for fear of hurting *his* feelings. By encouraging your child to share his feelings, and to be direct in expressing them, you will have a better understanding of his needs, and hopefully respond accordingly. If you listen to your child and accept his feelings, he will be likely to continue expressing them in the future.

It's also important to pay attention to unspoken feelings. Many children, especially young ones, cannot express their feelings in words. Some children, especially school-age children, worry about hurting their parent's feelings, and as a result, keep their feelings to themselves. When children don't express their feelings verbally, parents must look for more subtle clues in order to discover what they are feeling.

Kevin couldn't express his feelings in words. Instead, he expressed himself by acting bossy. His parents, unable to understand and separate their feelings from his, could not understand his behavior and the emotions behind it.

In contrast, while Caitlin did not verbally express her need to take her possessions from one house to the other, her parents understood the anxiety she was experiencing and her need for her teddy bear that provided comfort no matter where she was. Caitlin's parents paid attention to her behavior and responded in a way that served her needs by letting her take "Teddy" — her transitional object — between houses. Even if your child doesn't express her feelings verbally, you must make every effort to understand the emotions behind her behaviors and respond appropriately. Doing so will increase your empathy for your child, a healthy trait.

None of the suggestions in this chapter are intended to say that your child should always have his way. Empathy for your child's feelings need not mean giving in to his wishes most of the time. Your needs are important too. Parents balance their own needs and their child's needs all the time. However, without empathy and an understanding of your child's feelings, and the ability to separate your own needs from your child's needs, it is hard to maintain that balance. Finally, in order to maintain healthy boundaries with your child, you will need to focus on being responsible for yourself, taking care of yourself, and understanding yourself, so you can then take care of him. We'll take a closer look at these tasks in chapter 8.

Things to Remember:

• Support your child's social life, activities and interests after your divorce just as you did before your divorce.

• Allow your child to take her belongings wherever she wants. Remember that transitional objects are important to her emotional well being.

• Share your child's time and participate in his life according to your parenting plan. You don't *own* your time with your child.

• Develop healthy boundaries so that you can separate your own thoughts, feelings, and needs from those of your child.

• Put yourself in your child's place and develop empathy for your child and her feelings.

• Balance your needs with those of your child, communicating your decisions with your child and showing that you understand his needs and wishes.

• Take care of yourself so you'll be able to take care of your child.

Parenting Responsibly
on Your Own

"Just because we don't agree, doesn't mean one of us is wrong!"
— Anonymous

WHEN YOUR MARRIAGE ENDS, you still need to take care of your children. Many parents, however, struggle with their own feelings of anger and sadness, as well as potential feelings of inadequacy, and this makes parenting a difficult task. When you were married, if you and your ex shared the tasks of parenting, it is likely that you had some parenting tasks that you did very well and others that you struggled with. Now, however, you need to do all of the parenting tasks when your child is with you, and you might not be as capable as you'd like to be. Parents in conflict, however, tend to externalize blame and avoid looking inward when problems develop. Rather than figuring out how you can parent better, you might become critical, blaming your ex-spouse for any problems your child might have, without realizing that it might be related to your own parenting. In trying to make up for the loss of the family unit, you may overindulge your child and try to buy her love. This is especially true for non-custodial parents, who often feel guilty about their limited time and involvement with their children.

Some parents seem to want to be friends with their child, losing sight of the fact that their main job is to provide structure, guidance and appropriate discipline. This may cause some children to may become manipulative, attempting to pit you against the other parent. They may also struggle to find ways to get you to interact with each other with the hope that you will reunite. It's easy under such circumstances for you to become insecure about your new role as a divorced parent. By doing the best job of parenting that you can, and taking personal responsibility for your job as a parent, you can meet your child's needs in the healthiest possible way.

Stop Worrying About Criticism from the Other Parent

One of the most frustrating things you may face in parenting after divorce is constant criticism from the other parent. Parents are at risk of being criticized about many aspects of parenting, including:

- when you put your children to bed
- what you feed your children
- your choice of activities with your children
- the manner in which you assist (or don't assist) your children with schoolwork
- your methods of disciplining your children.

It's common for criticism by the other parent to increase when hostility during the divorce increases. This criticism can take on many forms. Sometimes parents may question each other about their concerns. This is the best way for parents to interact with each other. More typically, however, the criticism comes in the form of derogatory or sarcastic statements made to children, friends, relatives, or professionals working with the family. When parents criticize each other, they are typically looking for sympathy in their battle against the other parent.

The most damaging aspect of such anger and criticism, however, is when you make negative statements to your children. Examples of such angry criticism include:

- If you throw a letter that you have received from the other parent to your child and say, "Here, read this! Then you'll understand why I can't deal with your mother!"
- Making derogatory statements about the other parent's parenting in an email to your child.
- Saying to your child, "No wonder you were so tired at school this morning; your dad never puts you to bed on time."
- Alec Baldwin, the actor, received considerable criticism when he left an angry voice mail on his daughter's cell phone. The message included criticism of his daughter's mother, Kim Basinger.

While parents often regret making such critical statements to their children, they also often feel justified in being critical. However, no matter how justified you feel in your anger, such criticism is clearly detrimental to your children. It's important to control your emotions and refrain from making negative statements about the other parent.

It can, however, be very difficult to be on the receiving end of such criticisms. If someone is questioning your parenting techniques, you will first want to stop and think about whether there is some validity to the criticism. For example, if you hear complaints about your child's bedtime routine, stop and think if you are acting in your child's best interests and putting her to bed at a reasonable time. If you aren't properly taking care of your children, it's important to recognize how you can change your parenting to benefit the children. Consider how a structured bedtime might guarantee that your child gets enough sleep for her activities the next day. By truly thinking about the criticism — and correcting the situation if the criticism is valid — you show commitment to parenting your child to the best of your ability.

However, after thinking about it, you may feel that the criticism is baseless. The key to dealing with baseless criticism is to ignore it. You teach your child to ignore teasing by other children; in this instance, heed your own advice. When you hear baseless criticism about your parenting, the only sensible solution is to ignore it. Say nothing to your child; don't become defensive or return the baseless criticism yourself — just ignore it. Thus, a two-pronged approach of *thinking* about the criticism and learning from your mistakes, in addition to *ignoring baseless criticism*, is the healthiest way to deal with criticism from the other parent.

If the criticism comes from your child, however, your job is more complicated. It is easy to get defensive and return criticism to the other parent, but that only serves to vent your anger and increase your child's exposure to the conflict. Ignoring the criticism without comment, however, may lead your child to think that the criticizing parent is correct. The best solution when faced with criticism that comes through your child is to ask her how *she* feels about the issue, respond to her stated feelings, and encourage her to *always* express her feelings to you about your parenting.

For example, your daughter says "Mom doesn't like it when you keep me out so late," and you respond by saying, "What does your mother know, anyway? She feeds you hot dogs and sodas!" Becoming defensive and critical yourself is damaging to your child. Instead, you can help your daughter by saying, "I'm glad you told me how your mother feels, but I'm wondering how *you* feel about it." This not only gives her permission to tell you anything that has been said to her, but also to express her own feelings. If you really *are* keeping her up too late and she's tired for school, she's likely to say something like, "Well, I like being able to stay up as late as I want, but I'm usually tired in school the next day."

Perhaps she will attempt to play each of you against the other by saying, "I hate bedtimes. I don't know why Mom makes me go to bed so early." When you respond by saying, "Yeah, your mom's so rigid" you are only adding fuel to the fire. Your best response in any situation is to follow up on your child's feelings and explain yourself. For example, you might say, "I'm glad we're having a chance to talk about your bedtime. If you're tired in school, we'll need to work on you going to bed earlier." This is a response that shows her you're listening to her need to get enough sleep at night.

The best way to end the conversation is to say something like "I know it is hard with two sets of rules in two different homes. It is important for you and me to talk about the rules so that we can make sure they work best for you while you're here. You need to know how I feel, and I need to know how you feel, so that your needs are being taken care of. You know I love you and I want to help you with anything that is difficult for you in this divorce." Stop and think about the impact of your parenting, respond to your child's feelings, and ignore the criticism from your ex-spouse. This will allow you to be an effective parent, and also help keep your child out of the middle of your divorce conflicts.

Take Self-Responsibility

The most effective way to be an effective parent is to take responsibility for your own parenting. Remember, as mentioned in chapter 2, the best way to parallel parent is to do the best job of parenting that you can, while ignoring your ex's parenting. While you might have thoughts and feelings about your ex-spouse and his abilities as a parent, your primary task is to be the best possible parent you can be during the time your child is with you. Rather than focusing on your perception of inadequate parenting by your ex, it is critical that you pay attention to your own parenting job and attempt to improve it. You may make mistakes, but you want to do the best job you can with your child. By focusing on your own parenting, you are showing your child that you love him and are working to parent him in the healthiest possible way. If you focus on blaming the other parent, you are teaching your child to blame others for problems in his life. The best way to teach your child to take responsibility for his own behavior is to model self-responsibility as his parent.

Modeling self-responsibility is hard work. It requires that you:

- avoid blaming the other parent
- question yourself to make sure you are doing a good job as a parent
- understand your own feelings and admit to your child when you've made mistakes
- remain honest and open in your relationships
- communicate with your child about the issues in his life.

Be a Parent, Not a Friend

When parents divorce, it is common for one or both to feel guilty about the breakup of the family. This guilt often causes parents to want to be a *friend*, rather than a *parent*, to their children. This is especially true for non-custodial parents who may have less time with their children than they would like. If you are acting as a friend, it may be difficult for you to discipline or set rules for your child. You will probably confide in your child too much, providing more information about your life than she can handle. However, if you are a *parent* rather than a *friend*, you will teach your children responsibility and structure. If you act too much like a friend, you are abdicating your responsibility as a parent. While parents have rules and structure, and encourage responsible behavior, a friend will be more likely to support immediate gratification, immature behavior, and irresponsibility.

One way to be a parent *and* a friend is to encourage your child to share his thoughts and feelings. Support your child's activities and interests, nurture your child, and be there in times of need. Often, the tendency on the part of divorced parents is to ignore the responsibilities of being a parent and just attempt to be a friend by taking your child shopping before doing homework, overindulging him with things that he demands (video games, cars, expensive clothing, etc.), providing few limits, and encouraging him to avoid the responsibility of maintaining a healthy relationship with the other parent. A responsible parent will avoid scheduling a trip to the amusement park on the other parent's weekend, while a parent who is acting like a "friend" will urge the child to join him on a fun outing, regardless of the other parent's scheduled time.

The responsible parent:

- sets responsible limits.
- teaches self responsibility.
- respects the relationship the child has with the other parent.

The "friend" parent:

- sets few — if any — limits.
- supports play and instant gratification rather than responsibilities.
- undermines the relationship with the other parent.

Disciplining and Loving Your Child

Parents instinctively know that their children need limits, discipline, and love. However, many divorced parents often "forget" about these needs. In general, the most effective discipline is given in a loving manner, and for children of divorce, this is especially critical. Research suggests that the healthiest form of parenting is parenting which is "authoritative." Authoritative parenting emphasizes nurturing and sensitivity to your child's feelings, while simultaneously providing rules, structure, and reasonable discipline.

Children whose parents have divorced may feel insecure about relationships. While adults understand that there are different kinds of love and that parents can fall out of love from each other, your child may worry if you will always love her. If your discipline is harsh, and not given in a loving manner, (known as "authoritarian" parenting] your child may feel insecure about your love. The most effective discipline techniques include time-outs, setting limits and providing structure, while expressing love on a regular and consistent basis. Rather than telling your child what she can't do, tell her what you want her to do and why you want her to do it.

Psychologists have known for a long time that discipline needs to be provided in a consistent, loving, and natural environment. Parents learn that natural consequences — where the *consequence* of one's behavior naturally flows from the *behavior itself* — are the most productive. Parents can't allow natural consequences for young children for such things as running into a street or touching a hot stove. In these situations, parents provide restrictions and external controls — loudly and firmly saying, "No, this is hot!" and stopping the child's hand as it is about to touch the stove, for example.

As your child gets older and develops her own better understanding of these behaviors, however, it is wise if you allow the natural consequences to follow her inappropriate behavior. Your child is more likely to *learn* from her mistakes if she is free to *make* the mistakes, and if the consequences for those mistakes make sense. A typical example of using natural consequences is to let your child go without or make her own dinner if she doesn't want to eat the family dinner. This is preferable to a power struggle about food.

In addition to using natural consequences, it is also important to teach your child to learn from his mistakes. You can model this when you apologize for your mistakes and help your child understand how and why you made them. For example, suppose you are frustrated with work and you yell at your child. When you apologize and explain that *your* yelling was wrong, and that your anger wasn't meant for him, you teach your child to take responsibility for his own mistakes. If your child is used to seeing you stop and think about your mistakes, and explain and apologize for them, she will learn to do the same.

Most parents want their children to get along and not fight too much. If your children see you and your ex constantly in conflict, they will model this conflict and be in conflict themselves. If they see you and your ex work out your differences, they, too, will learn to resolve their differences. If your children are fighting with one another, encourage them to stop and think about what caused the argument, and ask them to consider a different way to solve the problem. By talking out the issues, you can support your children in using verbal methods to understand their differences and resolve their conflicts. By seeing you deal with the other parent in this responsible way, your children learn healthy conflict resolution skills that they can put to use with their friends and siblings.

Another important aspect of discipline is setting reasonable structures in the home for mealtime, bedtime, school, work (including homework, household chores, and jobs), and play time. Don't overindulge your child because of your own feelings of guilt. Instead, encourage cooperation, responsible behavior, and healthy social interaction in your child. Be consistent in setting limits; say "no" when you mean it, and follow through. These are important steps in maintaining responsible discipline for your children.

The most important goal of discipline is *to teach, not to punish.* Discipline is an expression of your love for your child. Your child may feel insecure about your love simply because of your divorce. She may need to be told more often than children of non-divorced parents how much you love her. When you discipline your child, set limits and tell her "no," you must also express your love. Tell her you love her, hug her, read to her at night, listen to her feelings and needs, and support and encourage her relationship with the other parent. These are all ways that you can show your child how much you love her.

It is important to remember that loving and nurturing discipline will be much more successful than harsh discipline. If one of your goals is to teach your child how to interact socially and be responsible, you must let your child know how important he is. By disciplining your child in healthy ways, you are showing him that you love him. By showing your child love and positive attention, you reduce the need to punish him, and you can nurture his healthy development in social relationships.

Healthy discipline and authoritative parenting includes:

- using time structures and reasonable rules with your child
- setting positive limits
- using time-outs and natural consequences
- frequently telling your child that you love him
- talking with your child about his thoughts, needs, and feelings
- teaching self responsibility
- supporting your child's relationship with the other parent.

Healthy discipline *never* includes:

- lack of structure in the home.
- inconsistent limit setting.
- yelling, screaming, and calling your child names.
- blaming others for your emotions and mistakes.
- harsh punishment and discipline, such as hitting.
- interfering with your child's relationship with the other parent.

Avoiding Your Child's Blackmail

When parents divorce and their children spend time in two different homes, it is easy for them to pit one parent against the other. Your child might do this — maybe unconsciously — to encourage you and your ex-spouse to be in contact with one another in the hope that the two of you might get back together. However, your child can also become mercenary at times, demanding things from each of you. By saying things such as "Dad will buy me that computer if I spend more time with him," or "Mom will let me go to the dance even if my homework isn't done," your child is, in essence, blackmailing you. While children of non-divorced parents may do this by saying things such as "Sally's mother is letting *her* go to the dance," it is easier for children of divorced parents to pit one parent against the other because these parents tend to be competitive with each other.

It's easy to worry that your child will love the other parent more than you. You might worry even more when you set limits and your child pushes those limits. Remember, if your limits are reasonable and consistent, your child's love and respect for you, and her sense of safety and security, will grow. Keep in mind that limit-testing behavior is to be expected and may not be related to anything that the other parent is doing. Your child may try different ways to get what she wants and, just as she might use her friend's parents as an ally, she may use the other parent in the same manner.

As a divorced parent, however, you shouldn't respond differently to blackmail associated with the other parent than you would with the parent of a friend. If you do, your child is more likely to use such blackmail in the future. Be firm, maintain your limits, and listen to your child. Just as you'd deal with criticism from the other parent, the best solution is to ignore your child's blackmail, while still paying attention to his feelings.

For example, if your son wants to go to the school dance, and you've set a rule that he can't go to the dance until his homework is done, it is important to stick to your rule. Since a school dance is a reward for responsible behavior, it makes sense that a natural consequence of not doing one's homework would be to miss the dance. At the same time, comments such as "If you like it better at your father's, you can go live with him," may cause the child to feel abandoned, and does nothing to enhance your authority. Don't even consider the other parent's rules and limits. If you've made a rule and set a limit, stick with it. If you're willing to negotiate with your child or restructure the rule, talk with him about it. Make sure your child understands why you've made this rule, encourage and support responsible behavior on his part, and work toward resolving your differences. You might ultimately allow your son to go to the dance if enough schoolwork is done, and he's promised to finish it in a timely manner. Ultimately, don't fall trap to blackmail just because it involves the other parent. Instead, if you try and work out consistent rules with your ex-spouse, blackmail can be eliminated.

It is important for you to be flexible. If you set up rigid rules for your child, you increase the possibility of a power struggle where there are no winners. By having a basic structure, in which the rules are clear and the expectations are understood, consequences will make sense. If your child tries to change the rules, negotiate (depending upon the age of the child) and see if it makes sense to be more flexible in your approach. If your child is willing to compromise, and you can be more flexible, it is possible to accomplish what you both want. This teaches your child that you're willing to talk out differences, attempt to resolve them, and find solutions that work for both of you.

Ultimately, it is best if you have an initial structure and reasonable rules in your house, along with a willingness to be flexible. These standards will allow you to teach responsibility to your children, while maintaining self-responsibility as parents.

Things to Remember

Responsible parenting includes:

- acknowledging that you make mistakes as parents
- ignoring invalid criticism from the other parent
- communicating with your child about his feelings
- paying attention to your own parenting and attempting to improve it
- avoiding blame of the other parent
- being a parent more than a friend.

Healthy discipline includes:

- maintaining reasonable rules and setting responsible limits
- using natural consequences rather than punishments
- teaching and modeling conflict resolution skills
- encouraging healthy structures in your home
- remaining sensitive to your child's emotions
- expressing your love to your child
- avoiding your child's blackmail
- remaining flexible and avoiding power struggles with your child.

CHAPTER 8

Taking Care of Yourself

. . . Or You Won't Be Much Use To Your Children!

"Never ascribe to an opponent motives meaner than your own."
— John Barrie

WHEN YOU GOT DIVORCED, you likely began to have a difficult time dealing with a number of feelings that often accompany that life-changing event. Some common emotional concerns include:

- fear and concern for your child and fears about your future
- sadness and loneliness
- confusion as you make internal changes
- anger and jealousy.

By understanding your emotions and working on dealing with them, you will do a better job of taking care of yourself. When you take care of yourself, it's easier to take care of your child. This chapter will address these emotions, and encourage you to use your time away from your child to take better care of yourself.

Fear and Concern

Even though your marriage has ended and you may be experiencing an influx of negative feelings, you still need to take care of your child. Fear is common to all folks as they get divorced. You are likely to worry about money, whether you'll be loved again, how you'll manage your life, and your new independence. You may look forward to making your own decisions and not having to meet someone else's approval, but you may also be afraid of making wrong choices. Divorce causes many parents to lose self-confidence and, at least temporarily, feel that they aren't able to make good decisions. Many feel that since their marriage failed, they may make other major mistakes as well.

It is normal to be concerned about how your child will adjust to your divorce. You've probably read about the increased problems that children of divorce experience, and worry that your child will have trouble in school, become depressed, or have problems in future relationships. However, while the popular press focuses on the negative reactions in children when parents get divorced, it doesn't have to be that way. Most research suggests that resilience in children is the normative outcome to a divorce. Economic problems, high conflict, and poor parenting are correlated with children's negative adjustment to divorce. However, if you develop and maintain empathy for your child and her feelings, avoid conflict with your ex-spouse, and parent in a responsible way, you increase the odds that your child will adjust to your divorce in a healthier way.

You can reduce your fears and insecurities by maintaining your own support systems. You're fortunate if you have the support of your family, friends, and co-workers. Don't keep your fears bottled up; talk with your friends and family about what you're feeling. At the same time, don't burden your child by sharing your fears with her. Listen to her feelings and reassure her, then step back and reassure yourself. It's not unusual to be insecure and worry more than usual during the first year after your divorce. Counseling may help you regain your self-confidence. Set goals for yourself and focus on what you'd like to change. Positive thinking can truly help. Think about things you always wanted to do during your marriage but weren't able to accomplish. Join clubs and participate in activities that help you feel better about yourself. Remember, things will improve; it just takes time.

Sadness and Loneliness

When you've been in a relationship, it may be hard to be alone after the relationship ends. Maybe you felt alone and lonely *during* your relationship, and that's why you chose to get divorced. Or maybe you didn't want the divorce and are devastated by the change. This may be the first time you've experienced loneliness. However, you are not alone. Use your support systems to avoid being lonely now and recognize that you won't be lonely forever.

With all of your new responsibilities, however, you might find it helpful to spend some time alone. Use this time wisely to learn about yourself and your likes and dislikes. Take care of your physical needs. Exercise can help you regain your energy when you're feeling sad and depressed. If you can't afford membership at a gym, go for a walk at least three to four times a week. Practice yoga or meditation, which are wonderful ways to spend some alone time and grow internally. It's hard to be depressed and worried when your mind is active and your body is moving!

Anger and Jealousy

When it comes to parenting, anger and jealousy are the most destructive emotions, perhaps causing you to hate your ex-spouse. You may be unable to let go of these feelings because you can't forgive your ex-spouse. It is especially difficult if you feel you were dumped for someone else, treated badly during your relationship, or no longer feel loved. When you can't forgive, you stay angry, and this anger is apparent to your child. Recent research has shown that learning to forgive brings inner peace. If you can learn to forgive your ex, you will become less angry, you will feel better inside, and both you and your child will benefit.

Unfortunately, if you're like many divorced parents, your anger is likely to be expressed in front of your child. You don't want to hurt your child, but when your anger erupts, the fallout is damaging. Sometimes your anger is obvious — derogatory statements or arguing with the other parent in front of your child — or more subtle, such as when you tell your daughter that she doesn't have to listen to her mother. If you haven't learned to forgive, you may act in ways that are damaging to your child.

If you can forgive your ex-spouse, you will go a long way toward keeping your child out of the middle, and be better prepared to model skills of conflict resolution for your child.

If you have truly forgiven your ex-spouse, you will be able to communicate without arguing and bringing up problems of the past. Getting past the "couple conflicts" you've experienced for many years will allow you to focus on your child's needs — and on your own. If you are a forgiving parent, you can say "hello" to the other parent in public places, and act in a business-like way when issues need to be discussed. Forgiving parents treat their ex-spouse just as they would treat other acquaintances and business partners. Divorced parents who have forgiven one another are able to be partners in raising their children. Forgiveness is an important step for responsible, post-divorce parenting.

It is important to remember that if you remain angry at your ex-spouse, you are likely to continue fighting. Whatever the dispute, you will try to win. You must do everything in your power to stop the fighting and reduce the conflicts in front of your child. Use your parenting plan and a different style of communication to avoid conflict. Chapter 9 outlines alternative methods of dealing with disputes. You can use professional mediators, evaluators, and parent coordinators to talk about the issues away from your child. Learn to agree with each other and parent your child the best you can.

The key element is to eliminate conflicts in front of your child. It is difficult to be a good parent to your child when you believe your ex-spouse is a "jerk" or a "dead-beat." Recognize that your child loves his other parent and needs to feel good about that parent in order to feel good about himself. If you continue the war, your child will feel like a prisoner and torn between you and your ex-spouse. In an attempt to please both of you, he may become anxious, lose sight of what he wants, and try to take care of *your* needs. He may also tell each of you what you *want* to hear, rather than expressing how he feels. These emotions and behaviors are unhealthy for your child.

Taking Care of Yourself

Many parents have difficulty letting go of anger and dealing with emotions, but there is a meaningful life in store for you after your divorce. Take care of yourself and your needs. Use the time away from your child to explore and understand your own feelings. Keep a journal and try to understand what makes you feel angry, disappointed, lonely, worried, or insecure. Note the ways you've become emotionally dependent on your child, and work toward building your independence.

Use your time away from your child wisely. Spend the time with your friends and develop your interests, or renew the interests you had earlier in your life. A friend of mine started horse back riding again, and another began sailing, after a hiatus of many years. Ben took a course in wine tasting; Sophia decided to try a self-defense class; and Barb joined a book club. There are many opportunities; find one — or several — that work for you!

Enjoy your adult activities and relationships. Take a class you've always been interested in. Pursue single parent activities in your community, through your church or synagogue, or at your workplace. Develop your spirituality. Work on improving your self-esteem. Compliment yourself when you've completed a difficult task or done an effective job of parenting. Don't compare yourself with other parents you may think are perfect. Chances are they aren't. When you feel stressed, a regular program of exercise will help. Walk, jog, or do some form of exercise daily. Read a favorite book and develop a hobby you really enjoy. All of these activities can help you feel better about yourself.

How do you want to spend your next ten years? Develop personal goals and find ways to accomplish them. Focus on your career and take satisfaction from your accomplishments. Take vacations, with your children and also by yourself or with a close friend. Liz took a child-oriented trip every year with her daughters, and they all had a great time. However, she also took one long-weekend trip each year, and a ten-day trip every three years by herself or with a close friend. This schedule rejuvenated her, giving her more energy for her children and work.

Finally, when you are ready, begin to date. Be cautious, and think about what you are looking for in a dating partner. Are you looking for company or for a new life partner? Be sure you've allowed yourself enough recovery and personal growth time. Many divorced parents rush into new relationships that aren't much different from their relationship with their ex-spouse. Others may be polar opposites, but may not be any healthier. Rather than focus on what you *don't* want in a new relationship (such as the opposite of everything that you didn't like in your ex-spouse), think about what you *do* want! What are the personal qualities that appeal to you? Maintain your sense of humor, and make sure your new partner has one too, along with other qualities that are important to you.

Don't introduce a new dating partner to your children too soon. Try to arrange the introduction during a child-focused activity. Your children and your dating partner may not instantly hit it off just because the two of you like each other. Give your children time to develop their own relationship with your dating partner, and reassure them that you will continue to love and respect them. If you give your children time to accept your new dating partner, pay attention to their feelings, and remind them that they are still "number one," your children are more likely to come to accept your new partner.

If you have teenagers, don't "compete" in your dating life. Talk about your own dating carefully and discreetly, and avoid talking about or exposing your teen-age child to your sexual behavior. Remember, if you are too much of a friend with your child, it may confuse her and make it difficult to set healthy boundaries.

By taking care of yourself, and using your time away from your child wisely, you will do a better job of managing your emotions and reducing your anger. This will help energize you so that you can do a more effective job of caring for her during the time she is in your care.

Therapy and Parenting Classes

Some parents find that it is easier to learn to let go of anger, understand their feelings, develop personal goals, and distinguish between their needs and the needs of their child if they have help from others. Some folks have friends who can serve this capacity. Some friends, however, may not be objective, and may try to give you advice that is not helpful. Other friends may try to run your life based on their own feelings.

Instead of relying on your friends and relatives, you might find that counseling will help you examine and resolve the issues at hand. Look for a therapist who understands and will address issues of divorce and co-parenting, rather than just validate your feelings of anger toward your ex-spouse. Encourage your therapist to challenge your feelings and help you let go of your anger and unwanted hostility. Work with your therapist to help you separate your feelings from those of your child, and to let go of your fears and criticisms of the other parent. Ask your therapist to help you think about the criticisms you've received from your ex-spouse and to determine if they are accurate or not. Work with your therapist to help you understand your child's feelings, develop your skills of empathy, and communicate more effectively with your child. By dealing with all of these issues with your therapist — and not with your child — you will feel better about yourself and do a better job of keeping the conflicts and your negative feelings away from your child.

It can also be very helpful to take a parenting class where you may learn skills that will assist you in your parenting. Most folks do not like hearing criticisms about their parenting from their ex-spouse. However, you can feel more self-assured — and be more productive in your parenting — if you learn effective parenting skills. A parenting class can help you learn to discipline more effectively, provide routines and structures that support your child, and improve your communication and empathy. If you take a class designed specifically for divorced parents, you may also learn more about the impact of divorce on your child, and learn skills to help your child achieve a healthy adjustment to your divorce. The support of a group experience provides a safe environment for identifying your parenting weaknesses, while supporting and enhancing your strengths. More about divorce education will be discussed in the next chapter.

Taking Care of Yourself Includes:

- Understanding your feelings
- Managing your feelings
- Letting go of your anger and jealousy
- Developing a support system of friends and family
- Exercising regularly
- Engaging in introspective activities, like meditation
- Using time away from your child to focus on yourself
- Rediscovering your interests and talents
- Setting goals for yourself and what you want in your life
- Choosing a therapist who can challenge you to think about yourself and your feelings
- Taking a parenting class.

CHAPTER 9

Resolving Parent Conflicts

Parent Education, Mediation, Custody Evaluations, and Parent Coordinators

"Pick battles big enough to matter, small enough to win."
— Jonathan Kozol

YOUR PARENTING PLAN will very likely be sufficient for dealing with the problems that may develop in your divorce. It is not uncommon, however, for divorced parents to become stuck and have difficulty resolving some issues. There are four unique models for resolving conflicts between divorced couples:

- Divorce mediation
- Parent education
- Child custody evaluation
- Using a co-parenting counselor
- Using a Parenting Coordinator.

All of these interventions are designed to facilitate you getting more understanding of your children's needs and/or your role in any problems that might exist in your family. With this greater understanding, you will hopefully find a new way to solve your differences and your problems. It's important to remember that *all* families have problems that need solving. However, if your problems don't get resolved in a healthy way, they may create a great degree of anger and frustration, which is difficult for you and hurts your children. By finding a way to resolve your difficulties, you'll be helping yourself and your children to move forward after your divorce.

Each of these interventions is quite different. *Parent education* gives you the tools to better understand how divorce will affect you and your children, and guides you toward more peaceful solutions. If you need help formulating a parenting plan, you can work with a *divorce mediator*, who will encourage you to find your own solutions to your differences. In many jurisdictions this is strictly confidential and you control the outcome. In some jurisdictions, a mediator can make a recommendation to the judge if you can't settle on a parenting plan. By using these two interventions, you have the greatest control over the outcome of your divorce.

If you remain in conflict and can't settle your differences after mediation, you may be referred for a *child custody evaluation*. With an evaluation, you will have little control over the recommendations that the evaluator will make to the court. Ideally, you will understand why the evaluator made her recommendations and will go into court prepared to settle your differences. If you're able to come to an agreement after your evaluation, you will still have complete control over how you work out future problems once the judge makes an order for your parenting plan.

However, if you still remain in conflict — and perhaps ten to fifteen percent of divorcing couples do — you might need the assistance of a co-parenting counselor or a *Parenting Coordinator*. A co-parenting counselor will work with the two of you to try and help you resolve your differences and create your own solutions. If your conflict is too entrenched, you will more likely need the assistance of a Parenting Coordinator, who will take control and make the decisions for both day-to-day and major issues.

It's best if you can retain control over issues by trying to resolve your differences with education and mediation. If you can't, however, an evaluation and/or the assistance of a Parenting Coordinator can keep you from floundering and remaining in conflict with your ex-spouse. Remember that conflict hurts your children, and solutions from a professional are better than continuing your custody wars.

The rest of this chapter will focus in more detail on each of the four conflict resolution interventions. As you read about them, remember that your primary goal is to find ways to resolve your differences so that you can take care of yourself and your children.

Parent Education

Since the early 1990's, court services and private resources have developed a service focused on parent education for parents of divorced children. In some jurisdictions, these services are mandatory, and may be part of a larger court orientation program. They may also be available as a separate component outside the court system. Typical parent education programs teach divorcing parents about the psychological effects of divorce on children, the negative effects of conflict on children, and, if the program is court-connected, ways to understand and use the court process. The primary benefit of parent education programs is encouraging parents to share their experiences and learn about the needs of children as parents enter the divorce process.

In an increasingly growing way, some parent education programs have a service for children. For example, in the San Francisco Bay area, a program called *Kids' Turn* (www.kidsturn.org) allows children to meet in small groups to express their feelings about divorce. They learn about what they can expect from their parents during the divorce process. At the same time, their parents are meeting in small groups to learn about divorce and the effect it has on children. At the end of the six weekly sessions, children's feelings are shared with parents by examples of artwork and writings so the parents might understand how their divorce is affecting their children. A similar program operates in South Florida, titled The Sandcastles Program (www.educationprograms.com/sandcastles).

In general, children benefit from these groups by having an opportunity to share their feelings with peers who understand them. They learn to understand, communicate, and manage their feelings, fears, and vulnerability. Groups for children designed to help them express themselves and better understand their feelings about their parents' divorce have proven to be very effective.

The benefits of parent education are significant regardless of whether it is court-connected or private, and whether or not it includes a children's group. Surveys typically show a very high satisfaction rate with mandatory parent education programs, even with parents who were skeptical prior to their attendance. Parents typically benefit from learning about their children's needs and feelings. Research shows that parent education helps parents reduce their conflict and learn ways to keep their children out of the middle of the divorce issues. Both low-conflict and medium-conflict parents benefit from these programs. While the use of parent education programs is growing, unfortunately it is still only a small component of the court process.

For higher-conflict parents, some communities are offering a more extensive program of parent education following divorce. Such programs integrate the traditional curriculum (i.e., how divorce affects children and why parents need to keep children out of the middle of conflicts) with a more extensive curriculum focused on stress, communication, conflict resolution, and problem solving skills. These programs are often run over the course of 8–10 weeks and are run with a small number of parents in a group setting. One example of such a program is offered by the Oregon Family Institute (www.oregonfamilyinstitute.org/parentedu.php). Another program, developed under auspices of the Oakland County (Michigan) Circuit Court, is known as ADEPT (www.oakgov.com/circuit/program_service/adept.html).

If you are going through a divorce, or in need of such a program, try and find a parent education program in your community. If one isn't available, work with your courts, local mental health community, and local bar association to get one established.

Use of Mediation, Not Litigation

Since the early 1980's, parents have increasingly used the process of *divorce mediation* to help them resolve differences and reduce the scars of battle. Child custody mediation is a process in which parents work together to develop a plan for parenting their children after divorce with the help of a neutral third party. While mediation can be done privately, the use of court-connected mediation has rapidly grown over the last ten years. In many states, the use of such mediation is mandatory before parents can litigate custody issues. While there is still some controversy and debate about mediation with families in which there has been ongoing domestic violence, divorce mediation can be effective for the rest of families going through divorce. Research over the past twenty years has consistently shown general satisfaction levels with mediation and there is evidence that children adjust to their parent's divorce in a healthier way when their parents mediate disputes rather than litigate.

The mediation process is one in which parents work together to devise a parenting plan that is mutually acceptable to both parents. As mentioned in chapter 2, this parenting plan may be quite structured, specifying the day-to-day time share of the children, as well as plans for holidays, vacations, and other special issues. By working together in mediation to develop your parenting plan, you can avoid the battles that are so damaging in an adversarial process, and you might also include your older children in the decision-making process, thus empowering them in a healthy way.

By using mediation to develop your parenting plan, you can help your children avoid loyalty conflicts, and reduce their likelihood of feeling the stress of battling parents. Children may benefit by being included in the decision-making process, because they can express their feelings and know that you are listening to them. Mediation may also give children the freedom to have a say in their lives and contribute to the decisions that affect their lives. You can expect your mediator to follow the *Model Standards of Practice for Divorce and Family Mediation* that were published by the Association of Family and Conciliation Courts (AFCC) in 2000 (www.afccnet.org/resources/standards_practice.asp).

Courts that offer mediation provide their clients a great service. Research shows that mediation can reduce litigation over custody. When parents participate in mediation, they are likely to reach a settlement sixty to seventy percent of the time. Parents are usually much more satisfied with the process and results of mediation than with litigation. Most importantly, if you mediate rather than litigate your parenting dispute, you will have control over the parenting plan. In contrast, litigation results in a judge determining how you will spend your time with your children. As evidenced by greater satisfaction, increased mutual decision-making, and decreased hostility, mediation is clearly a healthier alternative than litigation. For parents who live in an area where court-connected mediation is not offered, private mediation services are usually available and are typically well worth the investment, especially in comparison to the alternative of litigation. Remember, you will probably save money and have more control over the outcome if you use mediation to create your parenting plan.

Approaching Your Mediation

First, approach your mediation with an open mind, and be willing to listen. Parents who are open and listen to the mediator and their ex-spouse are the ones who are able to reach a settlement and develop a mutually satisfactory parenting plan. Parents who believe there is only one solution to custody and visitation issues, who are fairly stubborn, and who generally refuse to compromise, will make it difficult to reach a settlement. If you come with an open mind, you can brainstorm options until you find a solution that works for everyone.

Next, come prepared with several options. Do your homework before mediation. Think about and write out your proposals so that you can refer to them in the mediation session. You won't want to forget to discuss something that is important to you in the mediation. (The book, *Getting Apart Together* (Kranitz, 2000), has useful agendas and forms that you may find valuable in guiding your homework.) Make sure you understand your child's needs and stay focused. Be aware of the impact of conflict on your child (review chapter 1), and how the impact affects his developmental needs (chapter 4).

Third, mediation is not the place to focus on the other parent. Mediation usually breaks down when parents argue about "he said — she said" issues. Your mediation session is not a place to re-hash your marital problems, but rather a forum for solving parenting problems after your divorce. Communicate about your child and your perception of her needs. For example, if you're concerned about the other parent's display of anger in front of your son, talk about your son's need for peace. If you're concerned that the other parent lets your daughter stay up too late, talk about her need for routine and structure. Be open to what *you* might need to change for your child's benefit, and avoid character assassinations.

Finally, bring a sense of balance and humor. Things may get tense during mediation. Maintain a perspective that balances your desires, the other parent's desires, and your child's needs. This may not be an easy goal. If things get tense, remember that you're there *for your children*, and you don't have to like your ex-spouse to make an agreement on their behalf. Take a brief time-out from the mediation sessions if necessary. You may need several mediation sessions to reach a satisfactory settlement. Listen to the mediator's advice and consider it. She'll most likely have your child's best interests in mind, even if you and your ex-spouse can't agree on what that is. Recognize that your mediator's job is to try to balance what your child *needs* and what each of you *desire*, while at the same time encouraging you to reach a parenting solution. If things get tough, sometimes a humorous — but not rude — comment can break the tension and help everyone get back to work. While you will want to hold firm to your beliefs and values, remember that there may be many ways to satisfy these beliefs. Brainstorming all options before deciding on the plan that is best is a key ingredient to any successful mediation. Ultimately, you need to be open to different ideas, work to satisfy your goals, and be willing to compromise to reach a peaceful solution on behalf of your children.

Do's and Don'ts for Mediation

Do:

- Focus on your child's needs.
- Think of the custody and parenting plan related to what is best for your child as an issue separate from other divorce issues.
- Acknowledge your child's special needs according to age, temperament, and development.
- Acknowledge the other parent's strengths and bring up only valid concerns about the other parent's ability to care for your child.
- Acknowledge that your child needs time with both of you, in a safe environment, implemented by a parenting plan.
- Go to mediation prepared with:
- a proposal for custody and a time-sharing plan.
- a calendar that identifies school holidays, your work schedule, your child's activities.
- a flexible and business-like attitude.

Don't:

- Don't punish the other parent by withholding your children.
- Don't go to mediation unprepared.
- Don't bad-mouth the other parent.
- Don't assume there is a standard plan that fits the needs of all children.
- Don't focus on your needs.
- Don't discuss child support or property when trying to resolve your parenting plan.

Child Custody Evaluation

If you and your ex-spouse find that you cannot agree on a custody and visitation parenting plan, even after mediation and other settlement efforts, you might be ordered to participate in a *child custody evaluation*. Briefly, a child custody evaluation is a process in which a mental health expert, often a psychologist, evaluates your family and makes a recommendation to the court for a parenting plan that is in the best interests of your child. This section will explain in detail what you can expect when you have such an evaluation, and how you can prepare yourself and your family for the evaluation.

In mediation you and your ex-spouse are encouraged to reach your own agreement about custody and visitation, and develop a parenting plan for your children. When you have a child custody evaluation, however, your evaluator will recommend a plan to you and the court. Rather than a settlement process like mediation, a child custody evaluation is a process in which the evaluator gathers information about you and your family and makes a recommendation based on that information. In an ideal situation, you and your ex-spouse can use that recommendation to reach a settlement, but if not, the judge can use the evaluation — along with other testimony — to make an *order* for a parenting plan for your family.

Typically, an evaluation is required when parents cannot come to an agreement. There is usually a specific issue or two that requires an evaluator to make a recommendation. It is fairly common for evaluations to occur when parents cannot agree on day-to-day custodial arrangements, or whether or not a move is in a child's best interests. A child custody evaluation is often required when there is a significant change in circumstances, such as the start of school for children, or their movement into adolescence. Sometimes parents agree that they do not wish to share custody equally, but each parent wants primary custody of the children. In those cases, an evaluation is useful in determining which parent has the healthier relationship and is better suited for primary custody.

More complex custody evaluations are done when parents allege alcohol or drug abuse, physical or sexual abuse, domestic violence, serious mental illness or other such problems against each other during litigation. In such circumstances, the courts will usually order an evaluation in an attempt to determine the truth about the allegations and to make recommendations in the best interests of the children.

In recent years, it has been determined that the best way to do an evaluation is to have a single, neutral and objective evaluator who is appointed by the court and hired by both parents. This helps to assure that the recommendations are truly in the children's best interest, and not serving the interest of the parent who hires his own evaluator. By avoiding multiple evaluations, you reduce the likelihood of your children feeling caught in the middle of the conflict. The healthiest way to utilize an evaluation is to answer specific questions, and not use them as weapons in the litigation war. Ultimately, child custody evaluations are most effective as part of the overall settlement process. As mentioned above, it is best if you can use the information from your evaluation to reach a settlement on the parenting plan for your children.

Just as with mediation, you can expect your child custody evaluator to follow the *Model Standards of Practice for Child Custody Evaluation* (AFCC, 2006) (www.afccnet.org/resources/standards_ practice.asp) or the *Guidelines for Child Custody Evaluation* published by the American Psychological Association (APA, 1994) (www.apa. org/practice/childcustody.html).

The Evaluation Process

While not all evaluators utilize the same process, there are certain things that you should expect in all evaluations. These include:

- at least two individual interviews with each parent.
- at least two individual interviews with each child over the age of five.
- observations of your child (at any age) with each parent.
- a review of court documents and other appropriate written information.
- contact with collateral sources, such as therapists, teachers, day-care personnel, and pediatricians.
- a written report with specific recommendations about custody and visitation, and which addresses all of the major concerns raised by you and your ex-spouse.

In addition, your evaluator might do psychological testing or use questionnaires that help provide additional information about your emotional functioning or parenting style. These additional techniques are commonly used by psychologists, especially in more complicated evaluations, as they are designed to provide further information that will help in her recommendations. Your evaluator might also include a home visit at each parent's home in order to observe the family in a more natural setting. Home visits are particularly useful with children under the age of six.

What Can You Expect from the Evaluator's Recommendations?

As you've seen from the discussions above, one of the main differences between a child custody evaluation and mediation is that the evaluator will be making specific recommendations about your family. The recommendations may fall into several categories, including:

- Custody and access recommendations.

- A parenting plan that outlines the time-share between the parents and how parents might deal with future conflict-resolution.

- Therapy recommendations for either of the parents and/or the children.

- Special recommendations focusing on issues — if they exist — of domestic violence, substance abuse problems, and the alienation of children. There might be a recommendation for an updated evaluation after treatment or a set amount of time.

- Parenting classes to help parents improve their understanding of their child's needs.

- A re-evaluation as your child(ren)'s developmental needs change.

Co-Parent Counselor

After they have managed to get a court order and a parenting plan in place, many divorced parents need to find ways to improve communication and cooperation with each other. Many of these parents benefit from co-parent counseling. Co-parent counseling is quite different from marriage or couple's counseling in that the only focus for the counseling is improving the co-parenting relationship.

Parents meet with their co-parent counselor on an as-needed basis, often weekly until things improve. You can expect your co-parent counselor to focus on the following topics:

- Your child's needs and emotional functioning;

- Improving the way you communicate with your ex, focusing only on your child and not on your relationship with one another;

- Techniques to resolve your differences in a peaceful manner.

Co-Parent counseling is for parents who

- have a moderate amount of conflict
- are amenable to looking inward and developing insight into their own role in any problems with their children or the other parent
- want to help resolve issues on behalf of their children.

Folks who resolve issues in mediation but still need help in managing differences are prime candidates for co-parent counseling. However, folks who are in significant high-conflict, who want to reconcile in their relationship, or who are unwilling to work together on behalf of their children are not good candidates for co-parent counseling. They may benefit from individual counseling to work on their own issues and utilize the assistance of a parent coordinator (see below).

Parenting Coordinator

As stated throughout this book, research has shown that the level of conflict between parents is a significant factor in a child's adjustment to divorce. In recent years, jurisdictions from California to Massachusetts have looked for ways to reduce the conflicts between parents and to assist them in the day-to-day parenting of their children. One method that has shown great promise is the appointment of a *Parenting Coordinator* to help solve ongoing conflicts between the parents. Depending on where you live, your parenting coordinator may alternatively be called a *special master, case manager, family court advisor,* or *wise person.*

By definition, a parenting coordinator is a professional who is appointed by the court to act like a judge and make day-to-day decisions for divorced families in conflict. In practice, Parenting Coordinators are typically mental health professionals or attorneys with significant experience in working with high-conflict families of divorce. While the main job of the parenting coordinator is to make decisions that help a family stay out of court, many parenting coordinators utilize a blend of skills to assist the family by acting as an evaluator, therapist, mediator, and parent educator. The skillful parenting coordinator will work with each family to help parents reduce their conflict, stay out of court, and meet their children's needs. As with mediators and child custody evaluators, the AFCC now has

Guidelines for Parent Coordination (AFCC, 2005) (www.afccnet. org/resources/standards_practice.asp).

The parenting coordinator has a multifaceted job that is part *detective* (as parents tell different stories, it is her job to try and understand the "whole truth"), part *educator* (she teaches parents how to understand their child's developmental needs, resolve problems, share their children, and move on in their lives following the divorce), part *mental health professional* (she tries to understand your feelings and attitudes about your experiences and your children's feelings about their experiences), part *judge* (she makes important decisions that affect your life), and part *advocate for your children* (their needs will be her first priority in the decisions she makes). She may need to talk with other professionals, such as doctors, therapists, or school personnel, and may need to meet with your children to understand their feelings and opinions. She may also monitor your compliance with court orders, especially if there are major issues such as drug testing, visitation interference, or other such issues. Her job is a complex and important one because of the issues — and possible disputes — between you and the other parent.

In order for a parenting coordinator to be effective, a degree of trust must be developed between you and your parenting coordinator. By the time a parenting coordinator is appointed, you may be very distrustful of the court system and everyone associated with it. You probably already will have been through a custody evaluation, and both you and your ex-spouse may be unhappy with the custody arrangement established by the court. With this in mind, the parenting coordinator's first task will be to develop a sense of trust with you and your ex-spouse. This can best be accomplished with an individual, face-to-face appointment with each parent, where the issues are frankly discussed and your feelings are heard. The parenting coordinator will probably begin by explaining how she will be making decisions on behalf of your children. By encouraging you to trust that her decisions are in the best interests of your child, a positive relationship can develop between each parent and the parenting coordinator.

You are likely to find that your parenting coordinator will be decisive. Just as young children often have difficulty sharing, divorced parents often have difficulty sharing their children. While your parenting coordinator needs to understand your feelings, it is more important for your parenting coordinator to make decisions that are quick and clearly in your child's interest, without taking a lot of time.

You can expect your parenting coordinator to make decisions by following this system: First, she will look to the court order for a precedent, and use that in making her decision. Next, she will look at how the issue affects your child. Since "best interests of the children" are paramount, if there is a clear way of determining what is best for your child, she will use that as the basis for her decision. Finally, if there is no clear understanding of how the issue will affect your child, and nothing in the order that gives the parenting coordinator some direction, she will probably try to make a decision based on what is fair for the parents, and alternate those decisions between the parents. By keeping extensive notes of her contacts, and a record of all decisions that she makes, it will be easy for her to determine what's fair.

If you have a parenting coordinator, your responsibility is to keep her informed of your concerns. If you have questions about the parenting coordinator process, her understanding of your family situation, or concerns about the other parent, do not hesitate to contact your parenting coordinator.

Most parenting coordinators agree that you need to have the opportunity to do the best job of parenting that you can, without concern about the other parent's interpretation of your parenting job. You also need an opportunity for voicing concerns, and she is the one to voice them to. Another responsibility of yours is to follow the court's and parenting coordinator's orders, and act in a way that promotes conflict resolution and eases the pain and burden on your children. Keep in mind, whether working with a parenting coordinator or not, it's always important to make your best effort to promote a healthy relationship between your children and the other parent, and to avoid interfering in any negative way in that relationship.

It is likely that your parenting coordinator will try to help you understand why her decisions are in your child's best interests. Ultimately, your parenting coordinator's job is to help you and your ex-spouse accept your own responsibility to promote conflict resolution and ease the pain and burden on your children. Finally, it is likely that your parenting coordinator will be appointed for a limited period of time, such as one or two years, after which time you will hopefully be ready to resolve issues on your own. If not, you might find yourself re-appointing your parenting coordinator or looking for further assistance from the court in resolving ongoing issues. However, after one or two years, it is hoped that you will have learned new conflict resolution techniques and will finally be working together on behalf of your children.

Things to Remember

• *Parent education* programs are quite useful for teaching parents about divorce and its effect on children, and how important it is to resolve your differences away from your child.

• Use *mediation* to work together to improve communication, develop your parenting plan, and resolve your differences.

• If you still cannot agree on a parenting plan, use a *child custody evaluation* from a mental health expert for a recommendation.

• If you have moderate conflict and can try *co-parent counseling*, it can be a very effective process to learn improved styles of communication and how to focus on your child's needs and best interests.

• Finally, if your conflicts persist, and you cannot resolve your differences on your own — even with the help of mediation and co-parent counseling — you might need the assistance of a *parenting coordinator*, who can make parenting decisions on your behalf.

CHAPTER 10

Dealing with Special Problems

"I am convinced that life is 10% what happens to me, and 90% how I react to it."

— Charles Swindoll

THROUGHOUT THIS BOOK, the focus has been on conflict and its effect on your children, taking personal responsibility for your behavior, and doing your part to keep your children out of the middle of your conflicts. There are times, however, when you may be acting responsibly yet problems continue — more serious problems which require different interventions. This chapter will focus on three such problems: the *alienation of children, domestic violence and abuse*, and *dealing with a very difficult ex-spouse*. If you encounter any of these problems, you will probably need a child custody evaluation and a parent coordinator.

Alienation of Children

Jamie, eight, has been living with her mom since her parents' divorce nine months ago. During this time, her parents have been arguing over everything, often using her as the messenger in their war. She has become withdrawn and worried about her parents. Her mother is often depressed and her father is frequently angry. Both of them regularly say derogatory things about each other. She's torn between them, not knowing who to believe when they tell her different versions of the same story. In the last three months she has refused to see her father. Her mother, who's pleased that Jamie now understands how mean her father is, believes that Jamie is refusing to spend time with her father because of his anger. Dad, who doesn't recognize that Jamie is feeling anxious, believes she is refusing to see him because of her mother's negative behavior. As with everything else in their war, both parents are blaming each other, and neither is noticing that Jamie is withdrawing from her friends and feeling depressed. Jamie is becoming an alienated child.

It's an issue that has captured a great deal of attention in recent years. Alienation of a child — by one parent against the other — occurs when a child is coerced by a parent, either subtly or overtly, to form a loyalty to one parent and feel disdain for the other. This often occurs in bitter custody battles where children constantly hear derogatory messages about the other parent. Some are brainwashed and made to feel afraid of the other parent. Parents alienate their children against the other parent when they are hurt or angry with the other parent.

It is not alienation when a child has a history of being estranged from a parent due to abuse, neglect, or significant long-term personality conflicts. Instead, alienation always involves a pathological switch in which a child who previously had a good relationship with a parent is now refusing contact with that parent. During the last decade, the courts have seen an increase in the number of people claiming that the other parent is attempting to alienate their child from them. In order to reduce his anxiety, the child may "choose sides" between the parents. To complicate matters, many times both parents will act in ways that alienate the child. The important issue is how the child is affected by the parents' behavior.

Alienation is a very complex issue for psychologists and the courts to understand.[1] In spite of the complexity, you need to recognize that *it is always damaging* if your child is alienated and torn between you. A child's alienation is currently seen as an extreme reaction to your intense conflict. The damage may be short-term or long-term or both. The alienation may tear down your child's self-esteem. He may be more interested in taking care of your feelings and needs than his own, and it is likely that he will be depressed and angry. If alienation continues, his low self-esteem may be long-lasting, and there can be problems with authority and relationships, an unhealthy sense of entitlement, a tendency toward manipulative behavior, and difficulty with reality. By cutting off a relationship with one parent, he cuts off a part of himself, further affecting his self-image. Perhaps one of the most negative effects is found in the way he splits his emotions. Most alienated children are detached from their emotions — especially hurt and sad feelings — and may remain angry as a way of avoiding their feelings.

Your behavior can either promote or discourage alienation. Alienation can occur when you:

- talk in extremes and absolutes about the other parent.
- merge your feelings with your child's. For example, "We don't like the Tuesday night dinner visit."

- intrude on the other parent's relationship. Intrusive behaviors can include frequent phone calls (two to three times per day, or more) from one parent to the other parent's home during visits.
- encourage your child to act as a spy during visits to the other parent's house.
- inform your child about adult issues, such as child support, reasons for the divorce, etc.
- force your child to be the messenger of communications between you and the other parent.
- make derogatory and blaming statements about the other parent.
- include other family members or friends into the battle between the parents (sometimes referred to as "tribal warfare").

You can work to prevent alienation by:

- supporting and encouraging your child's relationship with the other parent.
- limiting your intrusive behavior when your child is with the other parent.
- doing a good job of differentiating between your feelings and your child's feelings.
- avoiding absolutes and derogatory statements about the other parent.
- communicating directly with your ex-spouse so that your child isn't a messenger or a spy.

Even if the other parent is promoting the alienation, you can limit your child's exposure to it by taking the high road, avoiding the arguments and refusing to be derogatory. While this is not an ideal situation, it is the better alternative.

How to Tell if Your Child is Alienated

Even if your child is exposed to inappropriate behavior and conflict between the two of you, if she is relatively secure with her relationships with both of you and has good self-esteem, she may not become alienated. On the other hand, she may feel insecure and anxious and have a difficult time with her feelings. She may be extremely torn by the conflict between you, causing her to react negatively to *any* conflict, and choosing sides in an attempt to reduce her anxiety.

If your child is alienated against the other parent, she is likely to have many of the following symptoms:

- She will make statements about "us," such as, "Dad's taking us to court."
- She will make superficial, trumped-up, exaggerated complaints about the other parent with no substance. ("Mom treats me like a prisoner!")
- She will make contradictory statements that may imply that she wants a relationship with the other parent. ("It's always so noisy here. Maybe I could at least get some peace and quiet over at Dad's house.")
- She will often repeat inappropriate information or make un-childlike statements. ("Dad's new girlfriend is such a floozy.")
- She will make character assaults & avoid answering specific questions. ("Why do you care how much ice-cream I've had? You're the one who's always on a diet.")
- She will show evidence of being used as a spy.
- She may be closer to the parent who is more insecure.
- She will probably describe things in absolutes — either all good or all bad.
- She will express fear of contact with the other parent, with no apparently sound reason.
- She may frequently be asked to keep secrets by the favored parent.

These symptoms are very damaging to a child, and reflect some serious psychological problems in the child and in the parent-child relationships. Most alienated children are angry, confused, and scared. When they express a refusal to see one of their parents, they often don't know what they truly feel, and their feelings are often merged with the feelings of their parents. For some of these children, their perceptions become distorted and they experience problems in many relationships. Clearly, these children are in need of individual and/or family therapy to work out their problems.

What You Can Do If Your Child Is Feeling Alienated

Once your child starts to feel alienated, it is critical to reduce conflict and urge your child to have a healthy relationship with the other parent. Remember that alienation is caused by your child's need to look at things as either "all good" or "all bad." In the example above, Jamie started to criticize everything her father did, and felt that her mother was "perfect." Psychologists refer to this as the child having "polarized feelings."

If your child is starting to respond to you as the favored parent, it is important to recognize that this is dangerous; try to help your child reduce those polarized feelings. Help her recognize the other parent's strengths and, at the same time, acknowledge your own weaknesses. Develop a sense of balance between you and the other parent. Your child needs to know that you value the other parent and her relationship with that parent. Support this relationship by encouraging your child to be with the other parent. Jamie's mother never encouraged her to go with her father, and secretly took pleasure that Jamie was becoming closer to her. As a result, Jamie didn't feel that her mother supported her relationship with her father.

When parents aren't in conflict they can support one another. When the child is upset with one parent, the other parent reminds the child that that parent loves him, and says something positive about that parent, becoming a buffer for the child's negative feelings. If your child is feeling alienated, become a buffer. Encourage your child to recognize that his other parent has value. Do all you can to keep your anger to yourself, and avoid exposing it to your child. Let go of your own anger and realize the benefit to your child in having and maintaining a loving and positive relationship with his other parent. Make sure your child spends some time with his rejected parent; you can't help your child heal his relationship if there is no contact.

If you are the rejected parent and your child doesn't want to see you, it is usually very difficult to know what to do. No one is supporting you and everyone seems to be against you. If you had a previously healthy relationship with your child, this rejection is very hard to understand and is emotionally painful. In spite of your temptation, never criticize the favored parent, as that will only make things worse. Encourage your child's positive relationship with the other parent, even though that parent is critical of you. Try to point out to your child that you understand how difficult it is for her to deal with all of this conflict. Stay sensitive to your child's feelings and help her balance good and bad feelings in other aspects of her life. This may be the only way to reduce her polarized feelings.

With alienated children, you might need to talk more about some of the divorce issues, but do so gently and carefully. If your child has a misunderstanding of the conflicts, start by saying something like this (adjusted as necessary for the age of the child): "I know it's real hard for you when you hear different things from your father and me. When your dad and I have such different views, I believe it's important for you to hear both sides rather than just one. I don't expect you to believe me, or your dad, but I do want you to know that there can be two sides to the conflict. I am real sorry that this conflict hurts you so much, and I sure hope you let me know what I'm doing to make things hard for you. I don't want to say anything bad about your dad; you can make up your own mind about who, or what, to believe. Just remember that I love you and that we've always had a good relationship together, and I want us to continue having that good relationship."

While doing some of these things might help, keep in mind that it is very difficult to know what to do or say if your child is feeling alienated. Get a therapist to help you with your feelings and a different one to help your child with her feelings. Use your therapist or your parent coordinator to help you figure out what else you can do to improve the relationship with your now estranged child. Finally, remember that you must never criticize the favored parent. If you have patience and give it time, hopefully you will return to a more normal relationship with your child.

As noted, you'll most likely need a therapist to help your alienated child sort out her feelings and reinforce a balanced view of both parents. Therapy may be critical in helping her to regain contact with her rejected parent. A thorough child custody evaluation by someone who is familiar with alienation will help you, the therapist, and the court to understand your child and recommend ways to help overcome the alienation.

If your child is dead-set against seeing or talking with the rejected parent, ask the therapist to monitor their initial contact. If *you* are the rejected parent, it is important that you acknowledge your child's conflicted feelings. Empathy — the ability to put yourself in someone else's place and understand their feelings — is very important at this critical step. Help your child understand that even if you don't agree with her, you understand her predicament and love her. Encourage her to tell you what she's feeling, and ask the therapist to encourage her to listen to your feelings. Try to find a common goal, and try to negotiate how much time you'll spend with her. While you might want to resume a normal relationship right away, give it some time. Support the therapist and your child. Let them know you feel comfortable limiting your time with your child initially, as long as it can increase again over time. Have empathy for the tension and stress your child must be feeling, and avoid blaming the other parent for your child's feelings. I've seen countless examples of parents who are trying to understand their child's feelings, only to damage the relationship further by blaming the other parent for these feelings.

Keep in mind that some children refuse contact with a parent because of problems with that parent. Before claiming that alienation is present, consider whether you are the one causing those problems by examining your own behaviors and attitudes. Pay attention to if, or how, you and your child were previously estranged. Understand why your child feels as she does, and try to genuinely apologize for past behavior and to work with her to show her that you can change. Again, this may also require the help of a therapist.

Since there can be so many causes for alienation, don't look for a single solution, and don't think you can solve your child's alienation on your own. If your child is alienated, you'll probably need a parent coordinator. You may also need repeated evaluations as things change over time. Get help so that you can reduce your child's anxiety and help her feel more balanced in her relationship with both of you. Remember, your child will experience fewer relationship problems as an adult if she can have healthy relationships with both parents now.

Domestic Violence and Abuse

Parenting is difficult, and everyone becomes angry and frustrated at times. However, *there is no excuse for violence or child abuse*. No matter how much you feel overwhelmed with being a parent, or provoked by the other parent, violent behaviors are unhealthy for your family and will not be tolerated by the courts. Too much conflict is damaging to your child and, when conflict is mixed with domestic violence or child abuse, it can be physically and mentally disturbing in the extreme.

Family violence can take on many forms. Depending on the research being cited, it appears that at least thirty-five to fifty percent of divorcing families experience some minor violence that occurs around the time of separation. While harmful to children, this is not the violence I'm referring to in this section. Instead, I'm focusing on family violence in which adults and children are abused by partners or parents on a frequent and consistent basis. This can take the form of what is referred to in the literature as "Common Couple's Violence" or "Situational Couple's Violence." While those types of violence can be quite damaging to children, it is not as damaging as the kind of violence that is often referred to as "Intimate Terrorism," in which one parent systematically and chronically uses physical and emotional violence, along with economic and sexual violence, to control the other parent in a relationship. Intimate Terrorism is the most damaging of all.

Research on violence has estimated that a minimum of three million children in the United States experience at least one incident of serious family violence in a given year. Other research suggests that a much greater number of children are at risk for witnessing family violence. Regardless of the exact number, it's clear that large numbers of children are exposed to family violence more than once or twice over the course of their childhood.

Children who experience chronic abuse generally feel vulnerable and insecure, mostly because the abuser's behavior is so frightening and unpredictable. Because parents use fighting and arguing, rather than reasoning, as a means of settling disputes, these children are likely to be involved in the power struggles. Adult victims of violence and their children live in a state of intimidation and fear which can be debilitating. They are at risk of being "hyper-vigilant," frequently looking over their shoulders and wondering what's going to happen next. Even if the physical violence has stopped, these children often continue to feel traumatized and anxious, especially if there are continued threats of violence or occasional acts of aggression. When there is a blend of psychological, physical, economic, and other violence that continues off-and-on over time, often with little or no apparent cause or warning, the abuse is perhaps most devastating and overwhelming to both victims and children.

Research has shown that children suffer the effects of short-term and long-term violence whether they have been the victims of abuse, or witnessed abuse between their parents. Children who are exposed to violence may develop externalizing symptoms and become bullies or violent themselves. They may also develop internalizing symptoms, and become fearful, inhibited, and withdrawn. Some children develop both internalizing and externalizing symptoms. They clearly are at risk of having more anxiety, more anger, and more problems with self-esteem and temperament than children who don't witness violence. These children are more likely to experience school problems and health problems. They are often detached from their emotions and have little awareness of their sadness, fears, and other insecurities. As teens or adults they may become abusive, fear that they will be treated abusively, or expect that they "should" be treated abusively. If your child has experienced family violence, it is your job to do everything you can to break that cycle of violence NOW!

Interventions for Families with Chronic Violence

There are three types of interventions designed specifically for divorcing families who experience violence and abuse. The first is structural and relates to the contact between the parents. You may have a restraining order that keeps you away from the other parent. Even if you don't have a restraining order, do everything you can to stay apart when you exchange your child. Make your transfers at a neutral site, such as a school or daycare facility as frequently as possible.

In instances where it is not possible to keep your distance, such as exchanging young children or during holidays or other special times, consider asking for assistance from a neutral person — a relative or trusted friend — to help with your exchanges. In many communities, supervised exchange sites have been established to help parents when no other solutions exist. At such sites, one parent drops the child off at the site fifteen minutes before the exchange is to take place and then leaves. The other parent then arrives at the designated time to pick up the child. In these instances, expect the court to make very specific orders. It's best if a parent coordinator is appointed to monitor everyone's compliance with those orders.

The second type of intervention relates to the visitation between the child and the abusive parent. If your child has been abused, and there continues to be a risk of abuse, supervised visitation with the abusive parent may be ideal. The supervisor is often a friend or relative, but professional supervisors are being used more commonly to ensure compliance with supervision requirements. Courts expect all supervisors to guarantee that they will remain attentive at each visit, and to alert the court if problems develop at any visit.

Courts are becoming more aware of how damaging violence is to children, even if they are not being abused directly, Violence is usually a reason courts limit contact between a parent and a child. Nearly half of all states have laws that limit a judge's discretion in granting legal or physical custody to parents who have abused family members. Nearly all of the rest of the states require courts to consider family violence as a factor in the development of custody orders. If the violence has been severe, the child may not have overnight visitation, and the contact with the violent parent might only be for several hours once a week, such as from 9:00 a.m. to 5:00 p.m. each Saturday. This limited relationship is designed to limit the child's exposure to the violent tendencies in the abusive parent and to protect the child from any future harm, while hopefully providing some positive time with that parent. On the other hand, if the violence was mild, has clearly stopped, and there is no evidence of current risk to the child, the time with the formerly abusive parent may not be limited at all. While joint physical custody may not be an option, if the violence has stopped, the child may have overnight and regular contact with the previously violent parent.

A third type of intervention is associated with treatment and intervention. Perpetrators of violence are often sent to anger management classes or batterer treatment programs, depending on the severity of the abusiveness. Anger management may be sufficient for parents who haven't had a history of serious abuse and where power and control are not the dynamics of the abuse. However, for chronic abusers, and for those with whom power and control are key motivators for maintaining the violence, the courts are increasingly sending parents to more intense batterer treatment programs, which may last up to a year. Adult victims of domestic violence are often sent to group therapy to help them recognize the signs of domestic violence and establish ways to prevent it. Children are often sent to individual or group therapy to help them deal with their feelings of vulnerability, insecurity, and fear.

Finally, it is important to point out that some perpetrators of violence can change. If they do, and if they demonstrate that the children are safe with them, they will often be given increased time with their children. If the victim is no longer in danger and the children are well cared-for, all of the non-therapy interventions described above can be relaxed, and a more normal relationship encouraged. Just as in families in which children experience alienation, you may need repeated evaluations and help from a parent coordinator to determine how things are evolving and how much risk still exists.

Dealing with a Difficult Ex-Spouse

It is an unfortunate reality that some people are very difficult to deal with. Psychologists who study human behavior describe certain personality traits that are extreme and create problems for others. Research suggests that a significant proportion of divorced parents who exhibit considerable conflict have some of these personality traits. Understanding and labeling these traits, and recognizing behaviors often associated with those traits, usually helps parents to deal with them. Most of the parents who exhibit these personality traits have a tendency to blame others when something goes wrong or things are not what they expect.

This section will focus on the traits I have observed to be most troublesome for parents and children of divorce, and ways to try and handle them. While none of these strategies is foolproof — you may need the help of a therapist, mediator, or parent coordinator to implement them — they might help you reduce your frustration. More than anything, though, these ideas are designed to help you deal with the problems yourself, rather than putting your child in the middle.

The Over-Reactive Parent. These parents may have fairly extreme reactions to observations or things that upset them. For example, when an over-reactive parent observes his three-year-old son having a temper tantrum after a visit with the other parent, he immediately wonders what went wrong during that visit. He will believe there is only one possible reason for his son's behaviors. He may worry about whether it is safe for his son to be with the other parent for such extended time. He fails to realize there might be alternative explanations for his son's behaviors. His son might be tired (through no fault of the other parent), he might miss the other parent, he might be having trouble adjusting to changes in his life, or perhaps something disturbing happened to the child immediately before the tantrum. Similarly, an over-reactive parent might get upset if you took your daughter skiing and if he felt you didn't dress her warmly or provide enough supervision on the ski slopes. Or maybe he feels you don't adequately help your child with homework, or that he doesn't get to bed early enough while at your house.

One of the things that makes dealing with an over-reactive parent difficult is that she may react so intensely. Additionally, she will blame you for things that she believes you did wrong. Finally, she is likely to leave angry voice-mail messages, faxes, or e-mails, or demand to talk with you about her perception of your "bad parenting." In more extreme cases, these parents go to an attorney, the court, or the parent coordinator with frequent complaints. All of this generates a high level of conflict.

A good way to handle an over-reactive parent is to have a sense of humor and a balanced perspective. The worst thing you can do is to over-react yourself. If you get an angry phone call or message, try to defuse it. Whether you believe it or not, you can defuse an issue by telling the other parent, "You may be right." Try and listen for a few moments and then offer to talk about the issue at a more convenient and appropriate time, *after* the other parent has calmed down. Set limits with the other parent if he becomes verbally abusive, telling him you'll hang up the phone if he doesn't stop. Ask if he has considered other alternatives for your child's behavior, or to explain in writing why he is upset with your parenting. As you do this, consider whether he may be accurate, or over-reacting, in his claims. If he's right, acknowledge it and indicate your willingness to modify your behavior. Thank him for pointing it out to you. If he's over-reacting, think to yourself "thanks for sharing." This can take the edge off of your own frustration. Realize that the other parent acts this way for a reason; perhaps he learned this trait from his own parents.

There is usually no need to manage an over-reacting parent by yourself. You might find it helpful to refer discussions about these situations to a third party who is balanced and doesn't over-react. Use a mediator, parent coordinator, or co-parenting counselor as described in chapter 9. One of the main tasks of the neutral professional is to take the pressure off of you, and try to help the other parent see how she has over-reacted. The neutral professional can carry the load of the frustration, and you can trust him to try and reduce the hurt to you and your child by these over-reactions.

The Rigid Parent. Some parents just cannot compromise. They find loopholes in the parenting plan and they demand that the other parent do what they want. For example, the parenting plan may state, "Mother and Father shall alternate Halloween. Mother has Julie in even-numbered years and father shall have Julie in odd-numbered years." The rigid parent demands that Julie come to his house on Halloween Day at noon and not be returned until the next morning. When you point out how that might be problematic for Julie because she has school on Halloween, the rigid parent doesn't budge. Similarly, you might want to take your child on a ten-day vacation, but the rigid parent won't agree because it interferes with his time. Even if you point out the benefits of the vacation, the rigid parent won't budge. He demands that your son make up the time, even though it will be more difficult than just giving up three days of his time.

Dealing with rigid parents isn't easy. You're probably tempted to become equally stubborn and resist compromise. The best way of dealing with a rigid ex-spouse is to have a thorough and airtight parenting plan. Use mediation or a child custody evaluator to develop the parenting plan. This makes it harder for the rigid parent to blame you should problems arise. If you have a clear parenting plan, it also leaves little room for disagreement after you are no longer in mediation. Recognize that you may have to develop a style in which you agree to disagree, and urge the rigid parent to use third parties to resolve what seem like unsolvable disputes.

If your ex-spouse makes a request you're willing to agree with, make it very clear when you agree to her request why you are agreeing, and how you think it benefits your child. This helps you stay focused on your child rather than the conflict. In the same way, if you are requesting something from the rigid parent, be very clear how your request benefits your child. Be prepared in advance for the other parent's rigidity. It might help if you put your request in writing, giving the rigid parent more than one option that she might agree upon. Try to keep the focus away from the two of you and strictly on your child. This is especially important if you are working with a parent coordinator or mediator.

The Self-Centered Parent. Some of the most difficult parents are extremely self-centered. A self-centered parent is likely to have little empathy for either you or your child. Chances are that the self-centered parent was also raised by self-centered parents, and no one considered his feelings while growing up. He has learned that he needs to protect himself by viewing all issues and conflicts surrounding *his* needs, rather than someone else's. Everything becomes personalized. If you're dealing with a self-centered parent, you're likely to be stuck in a battle between the needs of the self-centered parent and the best interests of the child.

Self-centered parents are the ones who demand overnight contact with a ten-month old, because "it's my right." Such a parent displays little empathy for the needs of a young child to feel secure by her attachment to a healthy parent. A self-centered parent may argue about how little league interferes with "my time." She is unable to understand how little league is a healthy experience for your child. A self-centered parent will be upset when your daughter's job gets in the way of the visitation schedule. He is likely to forget that her job is a valuable experience and helps her self-esteem. *His* wishes become more important than anyone else's and, lacking empathy, he will have little awareness of how his self-centered attitudes affect others, and in particular, his child. Some self-centered parents take an extreme position, refusing to see their children unless they have equal custody.

It can be extremely difficult learning to deal with a self-centered parent, and it may help if you can anticipate this behavior. If you expect it and can be prepared for it, you can respond in a way that you'll feel good about. For example, if you want to take your child on a well-deserved vacation, expect your self-centered ex-spouse to say, "Why do you have to be the one to take him on a vacation?" This is a response to some self-centered need of his. Rather than get involved in a battle, you can respond by saying, "Of course I don't have to be the only one taking him on a vacation. When would you like to take Nick on vacation?" While it's unlikely that such a statement alone will solve the problem, it is likely to decrease his resistance. If you add something such as, "During a different week or two, it's fine with me if you go on a vacation with Nick during the rest of the summer; I'm sure Nick would like that," his resistance to your requested vacation might completely disappear.

Similarly, if your daughter Ashley's soccer tournament is during your ex-spouse's scheduled time, urge *her* to take Ashley to the tournament and share in the excitement. Help her see that it's good for the two of them to experience the soccer tournament together. By trying to lower your ex-spouse's resistance, you might get her to agree.

It can be very difficult dealing with a self-centered ex-spouse. You should know, since you were married to him. It may be one of the reasons you divorced him! Don't blame him when he personalizes the conflicts, and don't complain about him to your child. Plan ahead when you want to make a request for any change in the parenting plan, knowing that he's likely to resist. Take time to consider his requests, so that you can respond according to your child's needs, not your frustration with his self-centeredness. As with the other difficult traits described, use your mediator or parent coordinator to help resolve more troublesome issues, rather than dealing with the frustration on your own.

The Constantly Angry Parent. Some parents, no matter how much time has passed since the divorce, remain angry. They become defensive when you question them, blame you for everything that goes wrong, and are unable to talk with you about issues concerning your child without getting mad. Their tone of voice is angry, and they yell at you, regardless of whether or not the children are nearby. When you are with such a parent in public, she might glare at you, especially if she thinks you are feeling good about yourself. She may also yell at you and bring up issues that she is unhappy about, creating tension for you, your children, and others around you.

While it may be difficult, do your best to try and understand your ex-spouse's anger and where it is coming from. If his anger is unpredictable and you haven't done anything to provoke it, it may be just a part of his personality; don't take it personally! Keep in mind that he may blame you for provoking his anger, but his feelings are not your responsibility. Very angry people rarely take responsibility for their own feelings. If he is angry that your new boyfriend is coming to your daughter's soccer game, recognize that he may be feeling threatened about his relationship with your daughter. Plan ahead and consider whether you even want to bring your new partner to the game. There's no need to provoke his anger needlessly. Maintain your inner balance. Use your sense of humor to tolerate and understand the angry outbursts and manage your own feelings. Never respond to his anger with more anger. That would only add fuel to the fire, hurting you and your children.

At the same time, don't be a doormat and let the other parent dump her anger on you. Be firm in your responses. If she yells at you over the phone, calmly tell her you won't be talked to that way and then hang up. If she tries to get you into an argument in public, remind her of the purpose of the public event (the exchange of your child or the soccer game), inform her you'll discuss the issue at a more appropriate time and place, and then walk away. If she threatens or harasses you, inform her you will seek a restraining order. If that behavior continues, *get* the restraining order.

You may very well need the help of the judge, a parent coordinator, or law enforcement to deal with an extremely angry person. You will want a court order that limits your exposure to her anger. You should expect all non-emergency communication between you to be via mail, fax, or e-mail. If she calls and it's not an emergency, tell her you won't talk, but urge her to let you know, in writing, what she called about. Hold onto your boundaries and don't let her cross them.

If you have lived with or continue to interact with an angry person for a long time, you will need to pay close attention to your own feelings and how that person's anger has affected you. Don't take it personally or let it affect your self-esteem. Remember, the other parent's anger says more about him than it does about you. Therapy may help you keep a balanced perspective of your own feelings and help you recognize how the other parent's anger has affected you. Therapy may also help you keep some boundaries in your life so that you aren't constantly overwhelmed by this anger.

Don't deal with the angry parent if you're not prepared to. Try to put off any meetings with the parent coordinator or mediator for a couple of weeks, and live your life without the distraction of that anger. Control yourself and your emotions so that you're better prepared to deal with him when you need to. Above all else, try to prevent the angry parent from drawing your child into the middle of the dispute, but even if he does, don't add to the problem. Try and withdraw as quickly as possible. If you have a parent coordinator, inform her and let her know that you're afraid he's putting your child in the middle. Then ask the parent coordinator to assist you in dealing with the issue at some other time, away from your child.

The Irresponsible Parent. Another particularly difficult parent to deal with is the irresponsible one. Often referred to as a "deadbeat" in the popular press, irresponsible parents don't pay child support on time, if at all, and often make promises they don't keep. They are constantly making excuses for themselves, and blaming others when things go wrong. They request last-minute changes, or simply don't show up for visitation. Their excuses are so common, even your child will begin making excuses for him. For example, when Anna's dad doesn't come to pick her up, she looks at her mom and says, "It's OK, he tells me he has to work late." She has heard this excuse so many times, and she knows it's not true; he either forgot, or got a better offer at the last minute. Since you were married to him, you're not surprised. In fact, it's probably one of the reasons you divorced him.

One of the more troubling aspects of dealing with irresponsible parents is the way they make *you* feel. When Anna's dad doesn't even call and let her know that he isn't going to pick her up, Anna is sad and angry. She may take out her anger on you, since you are the only parent available. Now you have to comfort an upset child, *and* change your plans at the last minute. You are furious! You don't want to dump your anger onto Anna, but it's hard to maintain your composure. You may want to make excuses to try and calm Anna. Of course, you wouldn't have to do any of this if Anna's dad had just picked her up — on time — as promised.

It's also very difficult dealing with your ex-spouse's lies and deceptions. When you call to find out about the late child support, she may not return your phone calls. When you finally reach her, you're likely to hear, "the check's in the mail," even when it isn't. When the check finally does arrive, it bounces, and she blames the bank. In court at a support hearing, she shows up with "copies" of the checks that she wrote, not telling the judge that the checks were no good, or not even sent. It appears that she puts more effort into avoiding responsibility than anything else. If your irresponsible ex-spouse spent half as much energy being responsible as she does making excuses and blaming others for her irresponsibility, there would be fewer problems.

One of the best ways to deal with an irresponsible ex-spouse is to modify your expectations and attitude. Many parents feel that the irresponsible ex-spouse is "getting away with it." At a certain level, this is true, but the irresponsible parent's life isn't good. He probably has few friends, receives little respect, and has little self-worth. He is likely to have poor relationships with people that matter (such as his children), to have very little stability in his life, and to be in trouble with credit agencies, courts, and others. You aren't the only one who has to deal with his irresponsible behavior.

In contrast, if you handle yourself responsibly and manage your emotions, you will maintain your self-respect and dignity. You will have to work hard to manage your emotions when dealing with him, but you will be able to take pride in your success, and your relationship with your child will be strong. Janet recently told me that her greatest accomplishment was never telling her daughter that her father was irresponsible. "I never referred to him as a deadbeat or a jerk, figuring it was best if she developed her own relationship with her dad and her own conclusions about her dad." While Janet had to work harder because child support was late or non-existent, she always felt good about herself. She now has a wonderful relationship with her adult child. By modifying her attitude and expectation, Janet succeeded in promoting self-esteem and emotional strength in her daughter. Interestingly, her daughter came to learn, on *her own*, of her father's failings. Despite her anger, she loves him anyway, but chooses not to see him very much because of his irresponsibility.

As you can see, it is important to contain your angry feelings. While this may be difficult, your child will be unhappy if you are angry all the time. Emily feels bad when her mom doesn't pick her up when she says she will. However, she feels even worse when her dad tells his daughter how irresponsible her mom is. His attempts to look like the "good parent" in his daughter's eyes leave her feeling frustrated and angry with both parents.

The Exclusive Parent. Some parents don't want to share their children. They see little value in the child spending time with or having a solid relationship with the other parent. These parents act as if they "own" their children. You'll hear frequent references to "my child," rather than "our child." The "exclusive" parent believes she should be the one to raise the child because she thinks she simply does a better job of parenting. While she may not blatantly alienate her child against the other parent, she will ask her kids if they really want to see the other parent, causing them to wonder if there's a problem with the other parent.

Exclusive parents believe they can move whenever and wherever they want. They usually have no concept of the potential impact of the move on the child and usually feel that whatever is good for them is good for their children. These parents typically have difficulty understanding the difference between their own feelings and needs, and the feelings and needs of their children.

Another thing that these parents often do is fill out emergency forms and other paperwork concerning the children as if you don't exist. They may name the step-parent as the second emergency parent, leaving you, the biological parent, out altogether. When mothers and fathers have different last names, some exclusive-parent mothers fill out school or extra-curricular paperwork as if the child has their last name, even though the child legally has the father's last name. This is harmful because it confuses the child and angers the father, who feels alienated by the mother. This is also very difficult for school personnel, who get caught in the middle of the dispute. *Never sign up your child for anything without using his correct first and last name.* Some of the worst conflicts in court are seen when one parent uses the wrong last name on the child's paperwork, or leaves the other parent off the school emergency cards, and then acts as if she didn't do anything wrong.

The only way to deal with exclusive parents is to hold firm in your relationship with your child. Don't let the other parent take over. Become as active as you can in your child's life, and try to develop special interests with your child. Go to the school and make sure your name is on the emergency cards. Develop your own, independent, relationship with your child's teachers. Leave a supply of stamped self-addressed envelopes for the teacher to send you important school information. Once you find out who your child's coach is, meet with him and ask how you can become involved and support your child. Check in monthly with your child's music teacher for a progress report. Don't let the other parent become the exclusive parent by default.

If the other parent wants to move, you can take legal steps to try to prevent it. Unfortunately, in many states, the law may allow such a parent to move with your child if he is considered a primary custodial parent. In other states, however, the parent who wants to move with the child may need to show that the move will benefit the child, not just the parent wanting to move. Many states now require judges to look at various factors associated with your child's best interests before allowing or not allowing the child to move. If the move is allowed, make sure that the other parent has a plan to encourage and support your relationship with your child. Stay involved no matter what the distance is between you and your child.

Greg lived in Northern California and his son, Scott, lived near Chicago. He had a weekly phone call with Scott's teacher, and talked to Scott on the phone three or four times per week. Once a week, they used a video-cam system to see and talk with each other, during which times they often played board games with each other over distance. During these calls with his son, Greg told Scott about his conversations with Scott's teacher. Every few months, Greg talked with the pediatrician and dentist and then let his son know he was paying attention to his medical and dental needs. Since Greg traveled a few times a year on business, he made sure that he could visit with his son as often as possible. Scott knew Greg loved him, and Greg's efforts kept the mother from claiming "exclusive ownership" of their son. On the other hand, if Greg's ex continued to interfere with Greg's efforts to relate to Scott, Greg would need to go back to court to force his ex to support and follow through on Greg's relationship with Scott. This can be very difficult to accomplish, so don't give up.

The Dependent Parent. Dependent parents come in three varieties. Some dependent parents seem to be continually asking *you* how to take care of the children. They don't want to make decisions, and are unsure how to parent. They may also ask for advice on finances, jobs, or relationships, or even for help with a trip they are interested in taking. Chances are the other parent was fairly dependent on you during your marriage and, if you let this continue, he may stay fairly dependent on you during your divorce. He may ask you about relatively minor parenting issues (for example, bedtimes, or how to discipline), not because he wants the routine to be consistent between the homes, but because he doesn't know how to do it himself. He doesn't really call you to talk about your children and how they are doing, but rather to ask you what to do. Over time, it feels as if you haven't even divorced him, since he is constantly seeking your help with the children.

The second type of dependent parent appears to be dependent on his parents or new girlfriend or wife for his relationship with his children. He is inconsistent in his visitation except when his parents want to see the kids and pursue it through him.

Since he's dependent on his parents — he might even live with them — his most consistent visitation is when he is with them. A relationship with a new partner can also affect this involvement with his children. Being dependent on his new partner, he wants to please her. If she wants to be with the children, he'll get involved with them. If she wants to have her own relationship with him, minus the children, he'll withdraw from them even further. In these circumstances, his relationship with his children is dependent upon how he is dealing with his other relationships. While this seems much like the irresponsible parent, it is different because he doesn't know how to maintain a relationship with his children on his own.

The third type of dependent parent is dependent on the children. While it is the parent's job to take care of her child's needs, this type of parent depends on her child to meet her emotional needs instead. Such a dependent mother will have a hard time when her children go to visit their father, and she will tell them she will miss them. She will let her child know how much she worries when he is at his father's house, hoping he will miss her. This causes her child to worry about her, making it difficult to enjoy himself at his father's house. He may even tell her that he doesn't like his father, not because it's true but because he feels the need to say something that will please her. When children take care of their parent's feelings rather than their own, they are referred to as "parentified." Your school-aged child is at risk of becoming parentified if he is anxious and insecure. Parentified children are at risk of rejecting a parent in order to please the parent whose feelings they worry about. Many parentified children have a very difficult time knowing how they feel, and have an even harder time expressing their true feelings. Instead, they are always worried about how others feel. As adolescents, they are at risk of developing behavioral and emotional problems.

It is quite difficult to deal with a dependent parent. If the other parent is dependent on you, you might want to allow it, since you know it will help your child. If she is dependent on a new partner or her parents, you will want to determine the impact on your child before deciding to do something about it. If her dependency on her parents results in "tribal warfare," as described earlier, you might want to work with a therapist or the parent coordinator to discourage it. However, if it leads her to spend more quality time with the children, you will want to support it. If the other parent is dependent on your children, however, you will want to do everything in your power to help your children to be emotionally healthy and less insecure. The children will need healthy emotional boundaries so that they can tell the difference between their own feelings and their parents' feelings. This way, even if your daughter acts somewhat parentified during the time she is with her dad, she won't be when she is with you. Since she'll feel less insecure and anxious, she will not be as affected by his dependency, and she'll hopefully learn how to separate her feelings from his.

The Over-Involved Stepparent. There's a good chance that one or both of you will get involved in a new relationship after your divorce. That new relationship can be a source of joy, or trouble, for yourself and your child. It may be hard to accept a new person in your ex-spouse's life, but it will be even harder to accept someone new in your child's life. If you have a new partner, you'll want to please your new partner and your child at the same time, which can be very difficult. The new stepparent might be confused about how to act and the level of involvement with a new family. While there are several good books written about stepparenting (see the appendix), there is one issue that is important to highlight: the over-involved stepparent.

If you are the stepparent in a new relationship, be mindful of the child's feelings and don't try to take over the parenting role. Allow the child time to define the parameters of your relationship together, and don't expect the child to love you instantly. In fact, she may never love you at all. Initially, try to be a good "friend," willing to support the child, listen to her, and help her sort out her feelings. Always respect the role of the biological parents, and define a role that is complementary to the other parent, as opposed to competitive. As long as the biological parents' needs are healthy ones, don't try to take over. For example, if your stepson loves soccer and his dad is the coach, be an active stepparent on the sidelines (unless the dad invites you to coach with him).

Remember that trouble often lurks in the small things. I've seen many arguments develop when the step-mom takes the child for his haircut, when the biological mom considered it *her* responsibility. Maintain your boundaries, and remember that you are the *step*parent.

Don't ask the children to call you "Mom" or "Dad." It's OK to have a special name, but it's better not to use the same name the biological parent is called. Let your stepchild define your relationship, decide what to call you, and support that choice. Joshua called his stepmom "Step" in a very endearing way. It reflected his respect for her, while not intruding on his relationship with his own mother. Though difficult to balance, a slight detachment is probably healthier than an intrusive involvement with your stepchild. Remember that the child's primary bonds are with her biological parents.

If you are married to the new stepparent, keep in mind your child's needs as well as your partner's, and be mindful of your own feelings. It can be difficult to support everyone's position in a conflict, so don't even try. Listen to your child if he is upset with your partner, but don't let him manipulate you. Keep in mind that your child's feelings are dynamic and likely to change over time. There may be times when he is very close with your new partner, and a moment later upset with her. Let your child know that his feelings are important to you and that it will take time to adjust to the new relationship. Encourage your new partner to allow the relationship with your child to develop slowly in order to avoid becoming over-involved. Talk about her role and how each of you envisions it. Your new partner probably doesn't know your children as well as you do, so it's important to help her understand your children and their feelings. Let her know what you think and how you feel. It's likely that step-parenting issues will be some of the more important ones for you to resolve. Again, there's no need to handle these on your own. Remember that you can use counseling to help you develop and maintain healthy relationships.

Things to Remember

• Children may become alienated because the pressure of their parents' divorce and the loyalty conflicts are too stressful for them.

• If your child is alienated and you're the rejected parent, try to think about how you can ease her conflict. Try to understand her feelings and anything you might have done to contribute to those feelings.

• If your child is alienated and you're the favored parent, recognize that the alienation is damaging to your child. Support his relationship with the rejected parent.

• Domestic violence and abuse are never acceptable forms of behavior. You have the right to be protected from abuse and violence. Get restraining orders when necessary.

• Children are severely traumatized by violence in the family, usually with long-lasting effects. Keep them away from exposure to any violence, and obtain emotional help for them.

• If you have perpetrated the violence or abuse, recognize that your relationships with your children will suffer and you may be limited in your time with them. Take an anger management class or other form of treatment to help you stop your violent behavior and understand its impact on your children.

• Some parents exhibit unpleasant behavior and then attempt to blame you for their unpleasantness. Learn how to manage your own reactions and use your parenting plan, parent coordinator, court orders, and therapists to help you respond to the other parent and cope with your own feelings.

• Avoid being an over-intrusive stepparent. Take time to develop your relationship with your stepchildren and maintain healthy boundaries. Avoid competition with the biological parents.

Notes

[1] For more information on the complexities of alienation, see e.g., Kelly J. & Johnston, J., The Alienated Child: A Reformulation of Parental Alienation Syndrome. *Family Court Review*, Vol. 39, No. 3, pgs. 249-266, 2001; Warshak, R. *Divorce Poison: Protecting the Parent-Child Bond from a Vindictive Ex*. New York: Regan Books, 2002; Stahl, P.M., Understanding and Evaluating Alienation in High-Conflict Custody Cases. *Wisconsin Journal of Family Law*, Vol. 24, No. 1, 2004.

CHAPTER 11

Dealing with the Courts

"The price of greatness is responsibility."
— Winston Churchill

FOR MOST PEOPLE, the process of getting divorced is a painful and difficult one. With no-fault divorce in most states, one parent may not wish to get divorced, but is forced into it because of the desires of the other parent. Yet even if both of you want to get divorced, and agree in concept on what to do, dealing with the courts may be more difficult than dealing with a conflicted marriage. Like visiting a foreign country where one doesn't know the language, divorcing parents enter a court system that is neither friendly nor easy, with a language and structure that is unique and difficult to comprehend. Given the costs and the frustration, many parents go into court representing themselves. Many of them encounter rules and language which is completely foreign to them. Others will hire an attorney, whose job it is to advise and protect your individual needs and rights, and run into a system that promotes litigation, arguing, and blame. With no-fault divorce and straightforward rules about child support and division of property in most states, the only thing left to fight over is your children. In the battle of divorce, winning custody often becomes more important than raising your children.

Adversaries Always Lose

The court process is typically an adversarial one, in which each of you is pitted against the other in a battle to see who will win. When you have children, the burden of an adversarial divorce is significant. Financially, you run the risk of losing your home, pension, and college savings in extended battles over custody. While the financial toll is most obvious, the emotional battle for you and your children can be even more draining. Since the adversarial system forces everyone to take sides, the resulting custody battle forces children to choose between their parents and makes them feel "like prisoners of war" (as twelve-year-old Alyse said to me). As the battle progresses, children become wounded, showing evidence of insecurity, problems in school, social withdrawal, and rebelliousness, all effects of a contentious divorce.

After the custody battle, one of you will have won custody of the children, but at what cost? By the end of this war, your children will likely experience increased loyalty conflicts, be afraid to love either of you for fear of hurting the other, and may feel afraid to talk about the other parent, knowing that it might anger or hurt the custody winner. In the extreme, your child may lead separate, completely different lives at each home, always being careful of what he says or talks about, in order to protect himself from the battle and his parent's emotions.

Even if it is not apparent to you, your child may experience significant problems. For example, if you are in the midst of a custody battle and can't attend your daughter's soccer game, your child loses out because she does not get support and encouragement from you. Worse yet, if both of you come to her game, but don't even say hello to each other, your child's attention may be diverted away from her game as she worries about protecting both of you in this emotional battle. Unfortunately, it is all too common for embattled parents to get into an argument during or after an event, causing the child to feel embarrassed, scared, or sick about the parents' behavior. Whether it be an athletic event, music performance, or school graduation, children of litigating parents are often afraid that their parents will make a scene and ruin the event.

By the time your battle is over, your financial resources are depleted, and the emotional scars are in evidence, it may be difficult to resolve your conflicts and effectively parent your child. The emotional aftereffects of the war remain with both the parents and children for years to come. The court process, and especially litigation, can damage families in ways that you may not anticipate. Not only do you lose but, as is evident, so do your children.

Hiring an Attorney

Before you hire an attorney, think ahead and plan your goals. You will want an attorney who will assert your rights in court *and* help you negotiate a fair settlement. In most cases, I encourage you to hire an attorney who will help you focus on your child's needs. Since there may be times when your rights and your children's needs will be in conflict, you will want an attorney who can help you balance the important issues.

Speak to several attorneys before hiring one. As you question potential attorneys, be aware of how well they communicate, and find out about their priorities. Try to avoid attorneys who urge you to fight for *all* of your rights without compromise; you're likely to pay more in legal fees without getting anywhere. Find out if your attorney is a specialist in family law. Family law is a unique field of law, and even though you might pay more for such an attorney, it's usually better to hire someone with a great deal of family law experience. Keep in mind the admonition "adversaries always lose," and try to find an attorney who promotes settlement and compromise, and who truly cares about children.

Ask a prospective attorney about her philosophy around issues of children's needs vs. parents' rights, and mediation vs. litigation. Contact your local bar association and ask for referrals. Finding out what associations your prospective attorney belongs to will help you can gain an understanding of her professionalism and philosophy. Members of the American Bar Association (or a local bar association) Family Law Section, or the American Association of Matrimonial Lawyers usually specialize in family law issues or may be a certified family lawyer. The Association of Family and Conciliation Courts (AFCC), is an interdisciplinary association of attorneys, judges, mediators and evaluators who are committed to improving the needs of children in divorce. Members of AFCC are likely to have a commitment to mediation and a concern for children. Many communities have family law attorneys who are appointed by the judge to represent children in high-conflict divorces. Even if such an attorney isn't available for your case, she may be able to recommend a colleague who cares about the needs of children. For more information on hiring an attorney, you may want to read *The Child Custody Book* by Judge James Stewart (see appendix).

Communicating with Your Attorney

Once you've hired your attorney, there are certain rules to consider in your communications. First, never lie or mislead your attorney. She can only represent you properly if you've told her the truth about your family and your situation. Since all of your communications with your attorney are confidential, you don't need to worry that what you say can be used against you. Even if there's something about yourself that might be embarrassing, you'll need to tell it to your attorney.

Make sure your attorney knows what you want. Speak clearly and avoid indirect or vague language. Feel free to tell your attorney "no" if she wants you to say or do something you're uncomfortable with. Remember, you and your attorney are a team, and as a team, you must work together on your behalf. Find out what your attorney expects of you and what you need to do together to reach a settlement. Ask your attorney questions and follow her advice. Be careful to consider her counsel, and if you don't understand or agree with her advice, talk to her about your concerns. If you still don't agree, tell her and let her know you want a second opinion. She's likely to encourage that. Again, don't keep secrets from your attorney or talk to a different attorney behind her back. By communicating your needs and listening to her advice, you can hopefully find a peaceful and workable solution to your divorce.

Acting as Your Own Attorney

Nowadays, many parents choose to represent themselves in court; there are many books promoting "do-it-yourself" divorce. Many individuals find that the cost of legal help for divorce is too high. While you might think you are saving money and aggravation by representing yourself, it may actually make things more difficult. Just like you *might* be able to repair your own car, a successful outcome is more likely if you take it to a mechanic. You might not have adequate knowledge to completely fix it, or it may take more time and cause significant aggravation for you to do it yourself. When I have a complex plumbing problem at home and try to fix it myself, it usually costs more and takes longer to repair than if I had called a plumber in the first place. Similarly, you might need an attorney even after you spent a lot of time trying to handle your own divorce.

If you still feel you want to handle your divorce by yourself, I would certainly encourage hiring an attorney as a consultant. While not formally representing you, a consulting attorney can help direct you, making sure that you are filling out the right paperwork and that you are getting a fair settlement. Learn as much as you can about child custody and property division, and be sure to carefully consider the tax implications of your settlement. You might be successful in representing yourself through mediation and settlement efforts, as long as you understand everything you need to know about your settlement. However, if you end up going to trial, you will probably need an attorney to represent you. Talk to your consulting attorney and see who she would recommend, given the nature of your case.

While courts in many jurisdictions have made it easier for self-represented litigants, it can still be difficult to understand the forms and the rules. If your ex has an attorney, you might be at a disadvantage if you go to court alone. My advice is to make sure you know exactly what you are doing, and hire an expert to represent you if you feel you are getting in over your head.

The Concept of Settlement

I hope it's clear to you that a main theme of this book is avoiding conflict for the sake of your child. As you deal with the courts, I urge you to avoid litigation and avoid the emotional and financial costs of a war. As Kimberly told me, "The best thing my mom and dad ever did when they got divorced was stay out of court." She was pleased that her parents had found a way to settle their differences rather than fighting in court. Her parents had developed a fairly thorough parenting plan, and then agreed to use mediation when things came up that they couldn't agree on. Settlement by the parents allowed her to adjust to the divorce and live a more "normal" life.

Judges also prefer that parents reach their own settlements. They don't encourage trials just so a parent can vent his anger or hurt, or to "have his day in court." Judges have seen the destruction caused when parents litigate and drag out custody and property issues, and recognize that trials can cause emotional and financial hardship. It's increasingly common for judges to urge parents to reach a settlement, rather than go to trial.

Trials lead to delays, and delays lead to conflict. You cannot go through a difficult trial and expect to communicate comfortably about your child the next day. It's difficult to have a working relationship with the other parent and coordinate the soccer games if you are in a war about custody and visitation rights. Reaching a peaceful settlement is critical. A court battle will increase the risk of problems for you, your ex-spouse, and your children. By all means, do everything in your power to *avoid the following:*

• *Family feud.* While the TV game show was entertaining, when friends, co-workers, and relatives get involved in your divorce, settlement becomes difficult. Everyone has a story and wants to take sides. Many people like to tell everyone they meet all of the bad things they can think of about their ex-spouse, allowing family and friends to rally against one another. Tribal warfare makes things worse for you and your children.

- *Making your children choose sides.* If you talk about your divorce and all its gory details, bad-mouth your ex-spouse in front of your child, tell her that she can't have a vacation because "Dad doesn't pay enough child support," plan special events on the other parent's weekend, or do something special (like go skiing) while your child is with the other parent, and then blame the other parent and the judge when your child asks why he didn't get to go, you will create conflict for your child. Even worse, if you demand that your child be with you because it's "your" weekend, even though she'll miss her last soccer game, your child will resent you.

- *Bringing up everything your ex-spouse did to hurt you.* Don't hold on to your hurts or exaggerate damaging events to make your point even clearer. Don't tell the judge your entire life story and about all of the lies and petty things your ex-spouse did to cheat or hurt you.

- *Fighting over your children to prove how bad your ex-spouse is.* Don't tell everyone that your ex-spouse has an alcohol problem or is a workaholic. While there may be a reason to seek primary custody because of your ex-spouse's problems, make sure your fight is worth it and important to the welfare of your children.

- *Demanding 50-50 custody because it's "your right."* Don't demand *more time* with your child just so that you can pay less child support, or demand *custody* of your child just so that you get more child support. Remember, your child doesn't care what percentage of time you spend with her; she just wants a healthy and positive relationship with each of you.

- *Being jealous of the new boyfriend/girlfriend.* Don't create scenes if Mom's new boyfriend shows up at your son's baseball game when you're there. After all, the bleachers are big enough for all of you. Don't tell your daughter that Dad's girlfriend can't take her shopping. If they do go shopping, don't tell her that her new clothes are ugly. Don't ask your children if Dad's new girlfriend "sleeps over," and then tell them how immoral it is. Don't make an issue of the new partner for the courts to settle. Also, if you're new in the relationship, keep some distance and don't try and take over the parenting.

- *Don't expect the court to solve everything.* Compromise on behalf of your children, even though only the judge can tell you what to do. Don't complicate the exchanges of your children. Have your kids ready and bring them back on time. Don't forget to feed your kids. Also, if they return to your home hungry, don't say anything about it before the next visitation. If you take your children out of town, tell the other parent of your plans. *Follow your parenting plan.* Don't blame the other parent to avoid your own responsibility. When problems arise, don't say to the other parent in front of your kids, "I'll see you in court!"

You can reduce your conflict and work toward settlement by doing the following:

• Learn to share your children, work to solve problems, and value the other parent's strengths.

• Avoid the family feud.

• Avoid putting your children in the middle.

• Avoid exaggeration.

• Let go of your hurts.

• Rather than fighting to prove how unfit the other parent is, be the best parent you can be without belittling the other parent.

• Remember that you can't solve the other parent's problems, but you can try to buffer your children against those problems.

• Learn to accept new partners in your ex-spouse's life and be happy if the new partner treats your child well.

• Follow your parenting plan, take responsibility for your own behavior, avoid blame, and use the conflict resolution techniques outlined in chapter 2.

Going to Court

Don't go to court unless there is no other option. Almost any decision that both of you reach on your own, even if you're not completely happy with it, is better than one which is forced upon you by a judge. Don't go to court because you are convinced that the judge will agree with your position; you could lose! Only go to court after settlement efforts have irretrievably broken down. Remember that going to court may be the most stressful thing you can experience in your divorce.

Some jurisdictions require a settlement meeting with the judge before a trial. If you still haven't settled, and you have to go to court for a trial, you and your attorney will need a goal that reflects fairness, compromise, and your child's best interests. Stay focused on your child and your relationship with him, rather than your ex-spouse and your relationship with her. Be prepared with a clear explanation of why your proposed parenting plan is better for your child than the plan proposed by your ex-spouse. *Don't use the trial as a place to bash your ex-spouse.* Rather than focusing on your ex-spouse's weaknesses, let the judge know about your strengths. You may need to acknowledge your weaknesses and what you are doing to improve them. Finally, don't expect the judge to simply accept your view of the truth without considering your ex-spouse's position. Instead, expect the judge to find a compromise solution that meets your child's needs and preserves everyone's rights.

Some parents return to court several times. This could be the result of constant arguing and breaking of agreements, or it could be because needs and circumstances change. If you need to make changes for your family, try to mediate and solve problems or disagreements before returning to court. Look for positive solutions to new situations. One of the more troubling situations leading to a return to court occurs when one parent needs to move out of the area and the parents cannot agree on new custody and visitation arrangements. Courts recognize that some parents have to move several times in their adult lives, and balancing the need to move with the needs of children is never easy. Rather than fight it out in front of a judge, try to recognize that your children will benefit if you make this parenting decision peacefully. Tough decisions don't have to be decided by a judge. If you are determined, you may be able to successfully mediate these tough decisions.

Finally, if you do go to court, do not expose all of the bitter details to your children. Never tell your children why you and the other parent are fighting in court; it only increases loyalty conflicts and makes them feel as if they have to choose sides. Avoid talking about the court issues within earshot of your children. (Remember, they're likely to overhear much more than you expect them to.) Don't take your child with you when you visit your attorney or to court, and avoid exposing them to the court proceedings. No matter how much you think it might help them to understand what is happening, it hurts them when they are exposed to conflict. While it's important to answer your child's questions about your divorce responsibly (see chapter 5), don't talk about the court issues unless your child asks specific questions, and then try to keep your answers brief.

Focus On Your Child's Needs, Not Your Parental Rights

It's unfortunate that the court process seems to focus on parent's rights. While the laws in all fifty states address the "best interests of the child," parents come into court talking about *their* rights. Advocacy groups — for men and women — tend to polarize parents and courts, furthering this trend. When you focus on *your* rights, you diminish the focus on your *child's* needs.

Instead, children have a handful of basic needs and rights that should be the primary focus within the court system. Children need to have healthy relationships with both parents, unless a parent has significant personality or behavioral problems, such as a history of substance abuse or physical or emotional abuse. Children need to have parents who cooperate with one another, share the task of parenting with one another, and treat each other as partners in parenting. They need to be free of loyalty conflicts and feel free to love both parents in whatever way they wish.

Use the courts to support your *child's needs*, rather than your *parental rights*. Ultimately, children need to be free to be themselves, as separate individuals, unburdened by your conflicts or expectations about their relationship with the other parent.

A Vision for the Courts of the Future (An Update)

In the original edition of *Parenting After Divorce*, I suggested ways to change the court system to improve things for parents and children. I wrote the following:

> "Decisions would be made more quickly so that parents and children can go on with their lives more quickly. Divorce would be less litigious, and when a judicial decision is needed, it would be focused on children's needs rather than parents' rights. Perhaps by studying and attempting to follow this "ideal system," you can achieve a healthy outcome for your child.
>
> In such a system, parents would be provided a variety of services. Like the information desk at a mall, you would encounter a *helper* who would listen to your concerns and direct you to appropriate services. The helper would refer you first to an *orientation class* to teach you about the process of divorce and

about your child's needs after the divorce. Then you would meet with a court-appointed *settlement officer* who could help you make temporary decisions. After this, parents would participate in a *court orientation process* and/or a *parent education program*. If your children are experiencing conflict and having difficulty, they would be served by a *children's education program*, as well. You would participate in *divorce mediation* unless you have already developed your own parenting plan. If you reach a settlement in the early stages of mediation, you would be done. However, if either of you raise significant concerns about the other parent, or if you need the assistance of an *evaluator* to reach a positive decision, then you would be referred to an evaluator. After the evaluation, you would return to mediation to try and reach a settlement, rather than going to court.

If you are among the very few families who still cannot reach a settlement, you would see a judge for a *settlement hearing*. By this time, the judge would have access to the evaluation and would encourage a settlement. Rather than litigation, judges would act first as mediators, directing parents into agreements in the areas on which they still need help. They would have a good understanding of child development in order to make rational decisions that benefit children's needs."

Since then, there has been a significant increase in the extent to which courts have utilized the services described above. As mentioned in chapter 9, there has been a significant growth in parent education programs throughout the country, with more programs designed to assist high-conflict litigants. There has been more research to show that children benefit from court-connected or school-based group intervention programs designed to help them normalize their feelings and learn to better manage their parent's divorce. More than anything though, the state of Connecticut has begun work on a triage process in which parents are directed early in their divorce process to services most likely to lead to settlement, or in the case of high-conflict cases, to evaluation services. Since that has begun, other states have inquired into the service and are exploring ways to potentially implement such triage services.

Even though my ideal is not yet in place in most of the country, by following the settlement guidelines throughout this book, real benefit will come to you and your children. You can become less litigious, learn conflict-resolution skills, and focus on parenting your children. Utilize mediation and evaluation when you cannot settle things yourselves. If you reach your own settlement, you can be at peace with each other, and you're likely to be more satisfied with the outcome and more likely to abide by it. By following these steps, you're less likely to be frustrated with the court process, and you will experience less pain, anger, and frustration at a time when healthier emotions are badly needed.

Things to Remember

• Court battles over divorce settlements and custody are expensive, emotionally exhausting, and rarely satisfying for either party. "Adversaries always lose."

• It's important to select an attorney who will help you get a fair settlement, but will avoid unnecessarily adversarial negotiations.

• Communicate openly and honestly with your attorney, including disagreement with her advice.

• Don't go to court unless there is no other option.

• Focus on your child(ren)'s needs, not your parental rights.

CHAPTER 12

Children's Thoughts and Feelings

"Pretty much all the honest truth-telling there is in the world is done by children."
— Oliver Wendell Holmes

IN TALKING WITH CHILDREN over the years, I've been struck by the variety of feelings children have when their parents divorce. My first significant experience in talking with children was when I researched joint custody laws in Michigan in the early 1980's. At the time, I was studying attitudes and beliefs about joint custody, and part of the research focused on the feelings of children and families who experienced joint physical custody. I found several families who had been among the first in my community to share physical custody of their children. The parents all agreed it was hard work, primarily because they had to remember where their children's things were and they had to communicate so much. However, all of the children that I interviewed for that research were positive about the experience. 10-year-old Danny told me "If all kids had the choice to pick what they wanted, I'd tell them to pick joint custody so that they could get to see their parents equal time. Being able to see Mom and Dad an equal amount of time makes up for moving back and forth." He went on to say, "I'd also tell the parents to stop fighting. Kids need both a mom and a dad, but the fighting has to stop."

In that same study, I interviewed judges, and one gave this prescription to parents: "If you really want to destroy a child, put him in the judicial system with a divorce battle that is going to last three or four years. If divorce is inevitable, get it over with in a few months, for everyone's sake."

Since that time, I have been interviewing children of divorce in many different contexts. I have been a therapist for some; an evaluator for others. I've interviewed many adults who were children at the time of their parents' divorce. Some were going through their *own* divorce, and many were reliving the feelings they had experienced as children. For purposes of this book, I also interviewed and questioned a variety of people — both children and adults — who have lived through divorce. In an effort to understand children's feelings about their parents' divorce, I discovered three major things: First, for many of the adults who looked back on their experiences of divorce, the questions rekindled some of the pain that they had thought was healed. They were struck by how much loss they still felt after ten or twenty years.

Second, the overwhelming sentiment was that the conflict and fighting hurt worse than the divorce, and conflicts and fighting *after* the divorce serve to intensify already painful feelings. These sentiments were near unanimous, and are consistent with my clinical experience and research with divorced parents and their children.

Third, many of the adults who responded to my questions had adjusted well to their parents' divorce. While it had been painful, many felt that their parents had done a good job in caring for them, in spite of the divorce. Along with this, both children and their parents had many suggestions for making divorce less painful for children.

My goal in this chapter is to provide the divorced parent with some understanding of what others have told me over the years. While I use a variety of questions in therapy and during evaluations, there were several basic questions used for this book that include the following:

- What has been the hardest thing about growing up with divorced parents?
- What have your mom and dad done to make growing up in a divorced family easier?
- What have your mom and dad done to make growing up in a divorced family harder?
- If you could encourage your parents to do (or wish that they had done) anything better as it relates to their divorce, what would that be?
- If you were real happy with anything your parents have done as it relates to the divorce, what would that be?
- What important things would you encourage divorcing parents to do to help their children?
- Anything else you'd like to share with readers?

During my evaluations and therapy sessions, I also asked adults who are now raising children of divorce to consider several questions. These questions included:

- What has been most helpful in allowing you to do a healthy job as a parent to your divorced child(ren)?
- What is your biggest regret as a divorced parent?
- What have your children said about how the divorce has affected them, both good and bad?
- What is the best advice you could give to other divorcing parents?
- What important things would you encourage other divorcing parents to do to help their children?
- Anything else you'd like to share with readers?

Answers to these questions have been grouped into various topics. In addition to the responses specific to this book, I have also included relevant statements from children and adults I have seen over the years. Names and ages of the respondents have been changed in order to maintain confidentiality.

As you read these statements, think about yourself and your feelings, and your children and their feelings. If you also experienced your parents' divorce as a child, think about your feelings at that time. Use this information as a guide to help you to better understand and relate with your own children and their feelings. What actions of yours match what children say they like, or dislike, about their parents and their divorce experiences? If you are doing things that children find hurtful, consider the impact on your own children and try to stop those actions. If you are doing things that children find helpful, continue doing them, and take pride in the fact that you are doing the best you can to help your children. To paraphrase Smokey the Bear, "Remember, only *you* can prevent divorce fires."

Communication

As mentioned in the chapter on talking with children, you can truly help — or hurt — your children by how you communicate with them about your divorce, your ex-spouse, or their feelings. The examples below illustrate some of the communication problems that exist between parents and their children. They are interspersed with examples that reflect healthier ways to communicate with your children.

"I wish my parents would talk to each other more about what I'm doing, how I'm doing in school and what they can do to help me, instead of arguing all of the time." (Jill, age 11)

Obviously, Jill is frustrated that her parents focus more on their arguing than they do on her interests and needs. Similarly, Brad, age 8, told me:

"When I told my dad I got a bird at Mom's house, he wondered why I have so many pets over there. Why didn't he ask me its name and tell me he thought it's great that I like pets so much?"

"Communication in the home is very important, prior to the divorce, during the divorce, and as we get older." (Joan, age 40, whose parents divorced when she was 15.)

Joan has recognized that she needs to keep the lines of communication with her children open, not only at the beginning of the divorce, but always.

"I hate it when you use me to play messenger. Just talk to each other and leave me out of it." (Brian, age 12)

This is a common complaint of children, who generally hate being the messenger of communications between their parents. They usually feel like saying, "Can't you tell each other, rather than me? Just figure things out yourself and then tell me; don't have me figure it out and tell you!"

"I'm glad they talk to me about how I feel, but I wish they didn't keep all of the divorce stuff a secret." (Steve, age 10)

While you don't want to burden your children with adult issues, they need to know basic details of your divorce and how it will impact them.

"They should talk to their kids more about the divorce. They should keep talking to their kids to find out what's working for them and what's not." (Kyle, age 13)

Kyle's point is that parents need to continue talking to their children about the divorce and their feelings, rather than assuming that once the divorce is behind them, it no longer needs to be talked about.

"My daughter has told me that how parents create the experience of divorce has more effect than the divorce itself. We talk about the divorce and how destructive divorce has been for her friends, so that we can handle it differently." (Paul, age 35, divorced father of two children)

Remember that your children watch and learn things from their friends, neighbors, and teachers. They're likely to compare how *you* handle things, and what they like and don't like with their friends and their parents.

Conflict

As I've pointed out throughout the book, one of the most damaging things you can do after your divorce is to remain in severe conflict with the other parent and expose your child to that conflict. Here's what some of the kids and parents have said on that subject.

"I wish my parents had gotten divorced sooner. They fought all of the time. Now I just wish they'd stop the fighting. It's like they haven't gotten divorced." (Tommy, age 10)

Tommy knows that the fighting in the marriage was unhealthy; he just wishes it would stop now that his parents are divorced.

"I hate it that every conversation with my dad starts with him saying, 'Does Mom . . . ?' They can't even be in the same room with each other without Mom saying, 'When you're old enough to choose who you want to live with, pick me!'" (Kylie, age 11)

Don't ask your kids about the other parent. It upsets them and makes them feel caught in the middle.

"My stomach hurts every night when my parents fight." (Aaron, age 6)

Many children experience somatic complaints when they don't have other ways to express their feelings. Needless to say, this is unhealthy for them.

"In my step-family, there was a lot of fighting and taking sides. My stepdad treated my stepbrother differently, and my mom treated me differently. They were always fighting. This was a mistake, and hard on my stepbrother and me. Even though my stepdad raised me, he was emotionally abusive, so I know I might have shut him out of my life more than I should have. I don't want to forget him, because he's still a part of me. I just wish the bad memories didn't outweigh the good." (Mark, age 16)

Children in your family need to be treated equally, regardless of "whose" children they are.

"The hardest thing for me is always feeling torn between both my parents. I feel like I can only please one or the other, never both. I

*hate it when my parents fight because it makes me realize that I
will never have a normal family. Every time my parents are in the
same room together, I can feel the tension and the awkwardness. I
just want to run away when they're together! The way they make me
choose one or the other is really hard on me. I hate the constant
schedule conflicts and court hearings. I just wish they'd leave each
other alone!"* (Elaine, age 16)

Elaine is expressing the feelings that many children have, namely,
that they can't please both of you. Don't make your relationship with
your child a competition with the other parent.

*"When my daughter was in the fourth grade, she had to do a class
project titled, 'What are your family traditions?' One of her answers
was 'going to court.'"* (Alicia, age 40, divorced mother of three
children)

Don't let this be a "tradition" in your family. Learn to resolve
your differences so you can stay out of court.

*"I hate having to choose sides. When my parents say bad things to
each other, they think they're hurting the other parent, but it really
hurts me!"* (Carla, age 14)

*"I hate it when they argue and criticize each other, especially with
their new partners. They're divorced; they should leave each other
alone and get over it!"* (Tom, age 15)

Recognize that your children often hear things, even if you don't
realize it. Make sure that your conversations with friends and new
partners about the divorce and your ex-spouse take place when your
children are out of the house, not just in another room.

*"Mommy and Daddy like to play tug-of-war, and Grandmommy, too.
Sometimes I'm in the middle and it hurts, and I cry."* (Natalie, age 4)

Things My Parents Have Done Well

While it's easy to focus on the problems of parents and divorce, many
parents do things well. Here's some examples:

*"They have done a phenomenal job of not putting my brother, sister,
and me in the middle. They are more than polite to each other most of
the time."* (Felicia, age 40, was 19 when her parents were divorced.)

*"My mom always respected my wishes to be close to my dad and spend
time with him."* (Mark, age 16)

"I'm glad Mom lets me take my favorite toys to my Dad's house." (Mary, age 7)

Mary feels more secure because her mom knows the importance of taking transitional objects and other favorite things between homes.

"They worked everything out by themselves and never went to court. Also, I'm glad that they never changed my schedule except for special occasions." (Adam, age 16)

Consistency and remaining conflict-free was important to Adam.

"I'm glad they only live five minutes apart. If I leave something at the other parent's house, they never argue about getting it." (Steve, age 10)

"Unlike some of my friend's parents, they've never been rude to each other in front of me." (John, age 14)

"I'm so glad that my parents try not to fight in front of me. One of my best friend's parents do that and it really lowers her self-esteem." (Katie, age 10)

John and Katie recognize that other adults aren't as healthy as their parents have been. It helps them feel better about their own lives.

"Letting me go to my dad's whenever I want, and not having a planned schedule." (Karen, age 7)

Karen enjoys the freedom to see her dad when she needs to. Not all kids like the routine of a schedule. It's another reason to talk to your children about their feelings.

"I'm glad they're still friends, even after they've both remarried, and we can all still get together socially for special events." (Joan, age 40, was 15 when her parents divorced.)

Things That Were Hard for Me

"I wish my parents had saved more money for my education instead of spending so much on the divorce." (Drew, age 17)

Battles in court are costly, both emotionally and financially, and many children have less money available for college as a result. Save the money for your kids.

"When my parents listened or interrupted me while I was on the phone with my other parent. When my parents made me feel guilty because I had made plans on their weekend." (Brian, age 12)

Children need privacy when talking with the other parent. You wouldn't interrupt when they're talking with their friends or another adult; don't interrupt when they talk to their other parent.

"I miss my daddy a lot and I don't like it because I want to see them both at the same time." (Nicole, age 5)

"When my mommy is at work and I don't see her for a few days. I miss my mommy and daddy when I don't see them all the time." (Adam, age 5)

Many children want their parents together because they miss an absent parent. Nicole and Adam might not feel this way if they saw the other parent enough.

"Travel between Mom's house and Dad's house. They live too far away." (Sherry, age 8)

Parents do their children a favor when they live close enough to one another for easy interaction with both parents.

"When I grew up, people didn't talk about divorce. My parents saw it as a failure. I remember telling my friends that a movie star was my uncle so that they wouldn't ask me about the divorce." (Phyllis, age 65, was 2 years old when her parents divorced.)

Many folks make things up rather than deal with their real painful feelings. Talk to your children so they don't have to make things up.

"My parents divorced because my dad was an alcoholic. I wish he would have stopped drinking." (Ashley, age 21, was 9 when her parents divorced.)

"I hate it when they talk bad about each other and have big fights right in front of me." (Steve, age 10)

"It's so annoying when they talk about the divorce too much. Don't tell my friends and their parents about it, because that's also so annoying." (Karen, age 7)

Many children get easily upset when they feel that their parents tell too many people about their feelings. Maintain your child's dignity. Don't tell everyone about your child's reactions to your divorce.

"My mother poured all her hurt, anger and bitterness onto my brother and me. My father totally absented himself from our family and started a new one." (Bill, age 32, was 12 when his parents divorced.)

Bill certainly missed his father and was angry at his mother for her actions during the divorce.

"My family is split in half by 2,000 miles. I enjoy my family here in New Mexico, but I often find myself thinking about my mom, my stepdad, my younger sister and all my other relatives I left behind in Pennsylvania. Each time I visit there, I have a wonderful time. It is too difficult to describe what it takes to say goodbye to my family in Pennsylvania and return to my home in New Mexico. My friends can never understand why I return subdued and a little bitter. The distance deepens the pain of the divorce since my mom is unable to share in my daily experiences. When I think about it, my mom doesn't really know me, and I don't really know her. It hurts to think about how much I am missing my sister's childhood, even though we have become friends. I wish I could have watched her grow up. I certainly wished my two homes weren't so far apart." (Mark, age 16)

"I'm mad that my parents' feelings are so bitter to each other that we can't spend holidays together. I hate it when they take their problems out on us." (Neil, age 12)

Neil is likely to grow up with painful holiday memories. Remember, holidays are important to children, and should be a time for creating special memories.

"I hated it when my dad didn't come to my baseball games and said it was because my mom was there." (Jeremy, age 11)

"Two things have been hard. Not having both parents available so I can talk to whoever I need to talk to. Also, separate rules in each house that I had to get used to." (Sam, age 10)

"I hate it that my parents live so far apart. That means I have to visit my dad on weekends that I want to be with my friends. It wasn't so hard when I was little, but now that I'm older, it feels like my life is torn into two separate worlds." (Michael, age 15, whose parents live two hours apart by airplane.)

"Since my father minimizes the large role he has in the pain my mother still carries, she hasn't let go of her pain and anger. I wish he had apologized to her long ago." (Felicia, age 40, was 19 when her parents were divorced.)

"When I was little, I never knew where I was going after school." (John, age 14)

Communicate with your child so he doesn't worry who will be there for him.

"When I was 12, my parents got divorced. They sat me down and asked me who I wanted to live with. I've wondered every day since then if I made the right decision." (Linda, age 28)

Don't put that kind of pressure on your child. Parents should make this decision together.

Advice to Other Parents

"Remember that you will always be connected. Learn to truly love yourself and your children." (Phyllis, age 65)

"Remember to keep your own needs and those of your kids separate, don't blur the boundaries." (Joan, age 40)

"I made a decision from day one that I would never badmouth Ron's father or tell Ron what he did to me. Don't put your kids in the middle. Never use them to get back at or manipulate the other parent. Allow your kids to make choices even if they choose the other parent and it hurts. They will respect you for respecting them. Set an example by taking the high road. Do everything you can so that your child grows up unspoiled, with generosity of mind and spirit. No matter how upset you may be at the other parent, don't take it out on your kid and don't let him see your anger. At his college graduation, Ron told me that some of his friends had to schedule separate parties since their parents couldn't speak to each other. I thought how awful and selfish that was." (Stephanie, age 50, divorced Ron's father when Ron was 5.)

"I think that the parent that has custody of the child, no matter the dislike for the other parent, should understand that the child does need to spend as much time with the other parent as possible. I think that once the divorce is final, that should be the end of conflict. A divorce can be hard enough for a child, and exposing the child to continuous conflict only makes it worse." (Brent, age 14)

"I'll recover from this divorce, but if I drag my kids through the recovery, they won't." (Lynn, age 41, divorced mother of two children.)

Lynn knows instinctively what the judge said at the beginning of this chapter; namely, that children can only recover from the divorce if they aren't dragged through the war.

"Work through your resentments with friends, family, and counselors, not your kids, and forgive the differences and betrayals that led to your divorce." (Paul, age 35, is a divorced father of two children.)

"Divorce isn't only hard on the family, but the community. Friends don't know where to place their loyalties. Divorcing parents need to make sure that their friends, and their children, don't have to choose sides." (Felicia, age 40)

"Agree with your ex that, no matter what, you won't use the children against the other. It only hurts the child and in the end erodes the respect your child has for the parent. It makes John (now 14) so happy to see us sitting together talking when we come to an event for him." (Terri, age 41, is John's mother.)

"My ex takes my kids for two days a week. This provides time for me to get organized. Single parenting certainly takes it out of you, and this 'rest period' is very healthy for me." (Mary, age 33, is a divorced parent of two children.)

Mary knows that she needs to stay healthy and positive in her life so that she can do a good job of raising her children.

"The child comes first no matter what. Don't use your child as a tool to get something out of the other parent. Child support is important, but holding your child back from seeing a parent due to a money problem is not the answer." (Carol, age 41, divorced mother of three children)

"I'd encourage kids to share their thoughts, fears and their sadness. Let them stay kids. Just because a parent is gone doesn't mean the child should have to step up to the role of partner, confidant, or caretaker. DO NOT TAKE THEIR CHILDHOOD AWAY FROM THEM." (Bill, age 32, was 12 when his parents divorced. He capitalized his message for emphasis.)

"Provide a united front and don't let the kids pit you against each other. And, never use your children as pawns. They are human beings, not pieces in a chess game." (Brad, age 35, divorced parent of two children)

"Hug your kids and play with them and tell them you love them." (Adam, age 5)

Good advice from a 5-year-old!

"I would encourage parents to stay friends because there is nothing worse than parents that can't stand each other. Think about your

children and how the divorce is going to affect them. Never use your children to get back at your spouse." (Elaine, age 16)

"Don't get a new boyfriend or girlfriend right away. It only confuses the kids and makes the other parent angry." (Jamie, age 13)

Take time before you start dating. Children need a period of adjustment before being exposed to new relationships. (And, for that matter, so do you!)

"Take care of yourself so you have the energy to take care of your children. Love your children and realize that they need normality. Remember that they love having friends over. Don't be afraid of admitting mistakes to your kids." (Alicia, age 40, divorced mother of three children.)

"I would encourage them not to put the other parent down, or try to make the kids play favorites. It is important to agree on things about my life so neither of them is mad at me." (Adam, age 16)

"Say yes to as many reasonable requests made by the other parent, even if it puts you out a little, and especially if it's better for the kids. Finally, don't move away. Live as close by as you can (but not in the same block) and don't consider moving out of the area unless you absolutely have to." (Megan, age 30, divorced mother of two children.)

I would like to add a statement shared by Lisa, who experienced divorce twice as a child: first when she was 3, and again when she was 15. Her words echo many of the ideas that I have tried to express in this book. While only 19 years old when she wrote this, I think her words reflect the wisdom we can all learn from. In a letter about her life and her parents' divorces, she wrote:

"I'm tempted to reprimand my parents for 'not thinking about their decisions harder or about their children,' but that's not right. I know they're great people, and human beings who make mistakes. God knows I've made enough mistakes. I'm only 19, so who am I to pass judgment or give advice? It is easy to pass judgment in hindsight, so I must emphasize that my parents and I love each other, and I hold no grudges against them. All I can say is that divorce hurts children more than their parents can imagine.

At times, the road with my parents was very rocky. I've seen it and lived it too much. About divorce, I want to say: Just don't do it! But that's not what this book is about. Instead, I can say this to parents: make the best of your situation with your children. Find the best balance possible between taking care of yourself and looking out for your children. Don't let your relationship with your children deteriorate when your marriage does. TALK to them. I've found that talking out our problems has been a great remedy for my mom and me. Your children have lost their family — don't let them lose you.

　　I am hopeful about my future. I see myself in a loving, stable marriage that really works. I want to get my faith and trust back. I've sworn to myself that I will NOT get a divorce. I know that at age 19 it's easy to think I have all the answers, but I'm not just idealistic — I'm tired of it all. I've had enough divorce for several lifetimes."

I agree with the statements Lisa has made, as well as her sound advice. Find it in your heart to talk with your children, support their relationship with the other parent, and help them heal from your divorce. From my own experience, and that of others, it may be your hardest, but most rewarding task.

Resources for Parents

Books for Parents

Ackerman, M. *"Does Wednesday Mean Mom's House or Dad's?": Parenting Together While Living Apart.* New York: John Wiley & Sons, 1997.

Ahrons, C. *The Good Divorce: Keeping Your Family Together When Your Marriage Comes Apart.* New York: HarperCollins, 1994.

Ahrons, C. *We're Still Family: What Grown Children Have to Say About Their Parents' Divorce.* New York: HarperCollins, 2005.

Appell, J. *Divorce Doesn't Have to Be That Way: A Handbook for the Helping Professional.* Atascadero, CA: Impact Publishers, 2006.

Berry, D.M. *Child Friendly Divorce: A Divorce(d) Therapist's Guide To Helping Your Children Thrive.* Manitowoc, WI: Blue Waters Publications, 2004.

Blau, M. *Families Apart: Ten Keys to Successful Co-Parenting.* New York: Perigee, 1993.

Bode, J. & Mack, S. *For Better, for Worse: A Guide to Surviving Divorce for Preteens and Their Families.* New York: Simon & Schuster, 2001.

Braver, S. & O'Connell, D. *Divorced Dads: Shattering the Myths: The Surprising Truth About Fathers, Children, and Divorce.* New York: Jeremy P. Tarcher/Putnam, 1998.

Dozier, B. *For The Children's Sake: Parenting Together after the Marriage Ends.* Lincoln, NE: iUniverse, 2004.

Einstein, E. & Albert, L. *Strengthening Your Stepfamily.* Atascadero, CA: Impact Publishers, 2005.

Everett, C. & Everett, S.V. *The Healthy Divorce.* San Francisco, CA: Jossey-Bass, 1998.

Fisher, B. & Alberti, R. *Rebuilding: When Your Relationship Ends* (3rd Edition). Atascadero, CA: Impact Publishers, 2006.

Hetherington, E.M. & Kelly, J. *For Better or For Worse: Divorce Reconsidered.* New York: W.W. Norton, 2003.

Hickey, E. & Dalton, E. *Healing Hearts: Helping Children and Adults Recover from Divorce.* Carson City, NV: Gold Leaf Press, 1994.

Johnson, W. & Murray, Kelly. *Crazy Love: Dealing With Your Partner's Problem Personality.* Atascadero, CA: Impact Publishers, 2007.

Kranitz, M.A. *Getting Apart Together: The Couple's Guide to a Fair Divorce or Separation* (2nd Edition). Atascadero, CA: Impact Publishers, 2000.

Lyster, M. *Child Custody: Building Parenting Agreements That Work* (4th Edition). Berkeley, CA: Nolo Press, 2003.

MacGregor, C. & Alberti, R. *After Your Divorce: Creating the Good Life on Your Own.* Atascadero, CA: Impact Publishers, 2006.

Mason, M.A. *The Custody Wars: Why Children Are Losing the Legal Battle and What We Can Do About It.* New York: Basic Books, 2000.

Neuman, M.G. *Helping Your Kids Cope with Divorce the Sandcastles Way.* New York: Times Books, 1998.

Ricci, I. *Mom's House, Dad's House: A Complete Guide for Parents Who Are Separated, Divorced, or Remarried* (Revised Edition). New York: Fireside, 1997.

Rothchild, G. *Dear Mom and Dad: What Kids of Divorce Really Want to Say to Their Parents.* New York: Pocket Books, 1999.

Shulman, D. *Co-Parenting After Divorce: How to Raise Happy, Healthy Children in Two-Home Families.* Sherman Oaks, CA: WinnSpeed Press, 1996.

Stewart, J.W. *The Child Custody Book: How to Protect Your Children and Win Your Case.* Atascadero, CA: Impact Publishers, 2000.

Talia, M.S. *How to Avoid the Divorce From Hell—and Dance Together at Your Daughter's Wedding.* Danville, CA: Nexus Publishers, 2006.

Wallerstein, J.S., & Blakeslee, S. *What About the Kids? Raising Your Children Before, During, and After Divorce.* New York: Hyperion, 2003.

Webb, D. *50 Ways to Love Your Leaver: Getting on With Your Life After the Breakup.* Atascadero, CA: Impact Publishers, 2000.

Books for Children

(Ages 4–8)

Brown, L.K. and Brown, M. *Dinosaurs Divorce: A Guide for Changing Families.* New York: Little, Brown, 1988.

Lansky, V. *It's Not Your Fault, Koko Bear: A Read-Together Book for Parents & Young Children During Divorce.* Minnetonka, MN: Book Peddlers, 1998.

Nightingale, L. *My Parents Still Love Me Even Though They're Getting Divorced: An Interactive Tale for Children.* Yorba Linda, CA: Nightingale Rose Publishing, 1996.

Ransom, J.F. *I Don't Want to Talk About It*. Washington, D.C.: Magination Press, 2000.

Stinson, K. *Mom and Dad Don't Live Together Anymore* (Revised Edition). Vancouver, Canada: Annick Press, 2007.

Wyeth, S.D. *Always My Dad*. (City unknown), Dragonfly Books, 1997.

(Ages 8–15)

MacGregor, C. *The Divorce Helpbook for Kids*. Atascadero, CA: Impact Publishers, 2001.

Pickhardt, C. *The Case of the Scary Divorce*. Washington, D.C.: Magination Press, 1997.

(Ages 9–12)

Blackstone-Ford, J., et al. *My Parents Are Divorced, Too: A Book for Kids by Kids* (2nd Edition). Washington, D.C.: Magination Press, 2006.

Blume, J. *It's Not the End of the World* (Revised Edition). Scarsdale, New York: Atheneum, 2002.

Stern, E.S., et al. *Divorce Is Not the End of the World: Zoe's and Evan's Coping Guide for Kids*. Berkeley, CA: Tricycle Press, 2008.

(All Ages)

Johnston, J., et al. *Through the Eyes of Children: Healing Stories for Children of Divorce*. New York: Free Press, 1997.

Krementz, J. *How It Feels When Parents Divorce*. New York: Knopf, 1988.

MacGregor, C. *The Divorce Helpbook for Teens*. Atascadero, CA: Impact Publishers, 2004.

Sample Parenting Agreement[1]

(Medium Level High Conflict Couple with School-age Children)

General Philosophy

1. Since we believe in the importance of both of us raising our children, we agree to share joint legal and physical custody of our children, Jeremy (currently age 8) and Jennifer (currently age 6). We agree to be cooperative in the best interests of our children. Because we have difficulty settling on many issues, we agree to the appointment of a mediation/arbitration professional, sometimes referred to as a Parent Coordinator.

2. Cooperative parenting provides a framework for our mutual agreement:

- to establish two homes for Jeremy and Jennifer;
- to arrange for the day-to-day care of Jeremy and Jennifer;
- to consult one another concerning the needs of Jeremy and Jennifer;
- to consult one another concerning our individual needs as they relate to Jeremy and Jennifer;
- to engage a mediator when needed to resolve our differences.

This framework does not require that any set method of parenting be used but only that it be established in a cooperative manner.

3. Both of us understand that cooperative parenting requires the acceptance of mutual responsibilities as well as mutual rights insofar as Jeremy and Jennifer are concerned and may require that we put their needs ahead of our own. We set forth the following agreement as to the times and places where Jeremy and Jennifer will reside, what our responsibilities will be, and other relevant factors. We further agree that this agreement will be reviewed at least on an annual basis and renewed or revised as necessary.

4. We are aware that the court always has jurisdiction to modify any arrangement that concerns the wellbeing of Jeremy and Jennifer. Notwithstanding this,

---

[1] Thanks to Robert LaCrosse, Ph.D., psychologist, Denver, Colorado, and William Hilton, attorney, San Jose, California, who originally developed aspects of this Sample Parenting Agreement.

we specifically express our intent to not resort to the court, except pursuant to paragraph 21e below.

5. While we were living together in a relationship, law and custom gave us certain rights and responsibilities regarding the parent-child interaction. It is our specific intent that these same rights and responsibilities continue, except as to those changes necessitated by the dissolution of our relationship and the establishment of two households. Since it was not necessary to be specific as to the exact terms of the parent-child interactions during our relationship, we do not feel that it is necessary to set forth all of the specific requirements of the new parent-child relationship. Such requirements as are set forth herein do not imply that this is a comprehensive or exclusive listing.

6. Both of us will continue to provide a home for Jeremy and Jennifer until they reach adulthood. Each of us will care for the physical, emotional, and intellectual needs of our children as best we can, and will have the best interests of Jeremy and Jennifer at heart.

7. We shall decide all issues between us, such as the time Jeremy and Jennifer shall spend with us, schooling, medical care, etc., using the general intent of this agreement.

8. It is agreed that the parent with whom Jeremy and Jennifer currently reside will have day-to-day jurisdiction of Jeremy and Jennifer; however, all decisions of a substantive nature (e.g., paragraph 9 below) will be made by consensus, if time and circumstances reasonably permit.

9. Major decisions pertaining to education, health, summer activities, and welfare of Jeremy and Jennifer shall be decided by both of us after adequate consultation has occurred between us about the developmental stages of the children, the welfare of the children, the best interests of the children, and, so far as possible, the desires of the children.

10. Both of us agree to foster love and respect, even in trying times, between the children and the other parent. Neither of us shall do anything which may estrange Jeremy and Jennifer from the other parent or hamper the natural and continuing relationships between the children and either parent.

11. We agree to honor one another's parenting style, privacy and authority. We will not interfere in the parenting style of the other parent, nor will we make plans or arrangements that would impinge upon the other parent's authority or times with the children without the express agreement of the other parent.

12. Further, we understand that each of us has or may establish an emotional/romantic relationship with another adult, and neither of us

requires that such relationship be a marital relationship, nor shall either attempt to limit the parental rights of the other solely on the grounds that such a relationship is not a marital relationship.

13. The personal possessions of the children are, as we both acknowledge, their personal property. They are to have complete freedom as to where they want their personal property: they may leave clothing, shoes, etc., at either of their homes, subject to a reasonable rebalancing of those items at periodic intervals.

Parenting Schedule

14. During the school year, as defined by the school calendar, the children will reside with their mother, except for the times noted below when they will be with their father.

15. During the school year, the children will spend time with father as follows:

a. Every other weekend, from Friday, when father or his appointee will pick the children up from school, until Monday morning, when he or his appointee will return the children to school.

b. Each week father shall have the children for a Wednesday overnight visit. This will begin immediately after school (after-school daycare may be used if pick-up cannot be immediate). The children will be returned to school by father or his appointee on Thursday morning.

c. During the last week each month of the school year, father shall have Jennifer on Tuesday from after school until the following morning when she will be returned to school. On Thursday of that week, father shall have Jeremy from after school until the following morning when he will be returned to school. As above, daycare and pick-up or drop off by an appointee may be used if needed.

16. School breaks will be handled as follows:

a. Christmas Vacation

- The vacation will be divided in half. The shift between households will occur at 12:00 noon on the appropriate day.
- Father shall have the first half of Christmas vacation in even-numbered years; mother in odd-numbered years.
- The parent who has the second half of the Christmas vacation will return the children to school on their first day back after the vacation, and the other parent's time will resume on that day.
- Christmas Eve and Christmas Day — see paragraph 17.

b. Spring Break

- Spring break shall be alternated each year, with mother observing it with the children in even-numbered years, father in odd-numbered years.

- Spring break will begin immediately after school on the day preceding the break. The parent who has the children during the break that year will pick them up.

- The children will be returned to school by the spring break parent on the first school day after the break.

c. Summer Vacation

- Summer vacation will be divided into two-week blocks. Father will have the first two-week block with the children, and mother and father will continue to alternate the children in two-week blocks of time until the end of the summer. Each parent can arrange his/her own day camp or such activities during his/her own time with the children.

- If away from home on vacations, both parents are obligated to inform the other parent as to the destination, travel route and flight information (if applicable) at least 10 days prior to the departure. These will also be filed with the mediator/arbitrator who will, at all times, hold the children's' passports until an appropriate release time.

- If the children are not traveling out of town, they will visit with the other parent one day per week, to include an overnight. The children, whenever possible, will be picked up from day camp and returned to day camp the following morning. If this is not possible, they will negotiate a comfortable, neutral pick-up and drop off with the final approval of the mediator/arbitrator. If the children are on a vacation trip, those days, of course, will not be observed.

17. Holidays and birthdays will be handled as follows:

a. Christmas Eve Day and Christmas Day

- To facilitate the holiday celebrations, Christmas Eve Day and Christmas Day will alternate.

- On Christmas Eve Day the children will be with the parent who has them for the second half of the Christmas vacation.

- On Christmas Day the children will be with the parent who has them for the first half of the Christmas vacation.

- When a transfer is necessary to implement this schedule, it is to occur at 8:00 a.m. and/or 8:00 p.m. as appropriate.

b. New Years Eve and Day

- The parent who has the children during the second half of the Christmas vacation will observe these days.

c. Easter Sunday

- Easter Sunday will be alternated each year, with father observing it with the children on odd-numbered years, and mother on even-numbered years. It will begin at 6:00 p.m. Saturday night, and end at 6:00 p.m. Sunday night.

d. Mother's Day

- Regardless of the normal visitation schedule, the children will spend Mother's Day from 9:00 a.m. to 8:00 p.m. with mother.

e. Memorial Day Weekend

- Memorial Day weekend will begin immediately after school on Friday and end on Tuesday morning after Memorial Day. Its observance will override the regular visitation schedule. It will be celebrated with mother in even-numbered years and father in odd-numbered years.

f. Father's Day

- Regardless of the normal visitation schedule, the children will spend Father's Day from 9:00 a.m. to 8:00 p.m. with father.

g. July 4th

- The day will begin at 9:00 a.m. on the 4th and end at 10:00 a.m. on July 5th, when the children will be returned to the scheduled parent. Father will observe July 4th in even-numbered years and mother in odd-numbered years.

h. Labor Day Weekend

- This weekend will begin immediately after school on Friday and end Tuesday morning when the children are returned to school. Father will observe the weekend with the children in odd-numbered years, mother in even-numbered years.

i. Thanksgiving Weekend

- The weekend will begin immediately after school on Wednesday and end with a return to school the following Monday. The weekend will alternate with spring break, so mother will observe it with the children in even-numbered years and father in odd-numbered years.

j. Parent Birthdays

- Parent birthdays will always supercede the regular visitation schedule. Since both parents' birthdays are during the school year, observation will begin immediately after school on school days and end at 8:00 p.m. On non-school days, the observation will begin at 9:00 a.m. and end at 8:00 p.m.

k. Children's Birthdays

- The children's birthdays will be observed with the parent with whom they reside when the birthday falls. The other parent will make alternative plans to celebrate the children's birthdays when the children are with him/her, according to the normal co-parenting schedule.

Parental Contributions

18. We will both contribute a share of our resources (money, time, energy, effort, etc.) to the children for their material and psychological wellbeing. Each of us will provide the necessary food, clothing, medical and dental care, shelter, recreation, etc., as would be usual and reasonable for a person in his or her economic circumstances.

19. Both of us agree to consult with one another concerning medical and dental insurance. We will determine which has the best plan for the best price and, if in agreement, obtain that plan. We agree to share the cost of that plan insofar as coverage for Jeremy and Jennifer is concerned. We further agree to divide and pay any uncovered costs on a 50/50 basis where such charges are less than $100.00. When such charges exceed $100.00 and are of a non-emergency nature, we agree to consult and discuss such costs.

Communication and Conflict Resolution

20. All communications about the children shall be written in a communication book, which shall move with the children as they pass between households. In it are to be noted important events of the previous week, the child's health and need for current medication, and upcoming appointments that may effect the children's scheduling. Requests for adjustments in co-parenting times may also be entered. While each parent is encouraged to respond to all requests within 48 hours, silence in regard to a request shall be considered a "yes." The book may not be used to criticize either parent's behavior.

21. Should any disputes arise between us or the children in the areas of education, health care, childcare, religious training, operation of a motor vehicle, extra-curricular activities, vacations, or other significant issues, we agree that it is in the best interests of the children and ourselves to resolve any disputes. All such decisions must be made jointly or arbitrated. They may not be made unilaterally by either parent. Should either of us wish to modify this agreement, we agree to:

a. Meet and confer with one another, each to present to the other a proposed solution to the dispute. If there is no resolution at this step, we will then:

b. Meet and confer with an expert in the field related to the dispute (e.g., doctor, teacher, counselor). If there is no resolution at this step, we will then:

c. Meet and confer with a mediator/counselor who has had experience in dispute resolution. All concerned shall use their best efforts to resolve the issues. Should there be no resolution at this step, we will then:

d. Submit the matter to a Parent Coordinator for mediation/arbitration prior to returning to court. If there is no resolution at this step, we will then:

e. Submit the matter to a court of competent jurisdiction. We understand that this is an extraordinary step and will be resorted to only when there is no other way to resolve the problem.

Miscellaneous

22. **Child Illnesses.** Whichever parent has had the children sleep over the night before an illness is responsible for staying home with that child the next morning if that child is too ill to return to school (or camp in the summer). Both parents are to inform the other of routine illnesses that require the child to stay home from school.

23. **Out-of-Town Travel.** If a parent travels out of town for fewer than 48 hours, that parent is responsible for arranging childcare for the children. If a parent is going to be gone for more than 48 hours, then the other parent must be offered first right of refusal. If that parent cannot care for the children, it is up to the traveling parent to arrange full-time childcare until his or her return. If a parent accepts care of the children, there will be no make-up time for the absent parent.

24. **Telephone Access.**

a. The children may call the other parent whenever they like, up to two times a day.

b. Each parent may call the children once per every 48 hours of absence. Children are to be given privacy for their telephone conversations. The call is to be placed at a mutually agreed-upon time (mediated if necessary, and to remain at the same time). The residential parent is obligated to ensure the presence of the children and the absence of any activity that may draw them away from the scheduled phone call (i.e., TV, neighborhood activity).

25. **Transportation.** The residential parent is responsible for delivering the child to the other parent and/or to the event or activity the child is expected to attend.

26. **Day-to-Day Decisions.** Decisions about bedtime, hygiene, minor disciplinary actions, minor medical and dental procedures, social events, activities, relationships, curfew, chores, allowances, social dress, and jewelry shall be the province of the household in which the child is currently residing. We both acknowledge the importance of consistency in these areas, and agree to communicate and cooperate whenever possible.

27. **Emergencies.** Each parent is required to notify the other parent within three hours of any medical emergency. The parent present is authorized to sign legal consents on both parents' behalf to permit emergency intervention.

28. **Information.** Each parent is required to set up his/her own information network for information about school and routine medical appointments. Each is required to tell professionals that they hold joint custody, and each parent has equal right to access all information. On any emergency information sheet, each parent will list the other as the first person to contact if he or she is not available.

29. **Geographical Relocation.** Relocation within the < city > metropolitan area (,   ,   ,   , and   counties) may be done only after mediation/arbitration has taken place as to the required changes in the children's schooling, daycare, and after-school activities. The children may not be removed permanently from <   state   > without the express approval of the other parent, a mediation/arbitration decision, or an order of the court.

30. **Review of Agreement.** During the month of June each year, the custody recommendations shall be reviewed and modified as agreed through mediation.

_____	_____
Father	Mother
_____	_____
Parent Coordinator	Date

NOTE: The examples above, while comprehensive, are not exhaustive in terms of recommendations, nor are they intended to be a "standard" agreement. Instead, they are intended to offer suggestions regarding the range of issues that must be covered and the depth of detail in which recommendations must be addressed for many families. I urge you to develop your own parenting agreement with the details and information required for your family with consideration of the amount of conflict that you normally experience.

Index

Rebuilding
When Your Relationship Ends (3rd Edition)
Bruce Fisher, Ed.D. and Robert E. Alberti, Ph.D.
Softcover: $16.95   304 pages
The most popular guide to divorce recovery. The "divorce process rebuilding blocks" format offers a nineteen-step process for putting life back together after divorce. Nearly one million in print.

The Divorce Helpbook for Kids
Cynthia MacGregor
Softcover: $12.95   144 pages
Discusses reasons parents get divorced; ways divorce will change kids' lives; kids' feelings about divorce; things kids can do to help them feel better; who to talk to; what's likely to happen next; life after divorce: visitation, custody, straddling two households.

The Divorce Helpbook for Teens
Cynthia MacGregor
Softcover: $13.95   144 pages
Friendly guide offers a helping hand to teens struggling to answer tough questions about divorce.

50 Ways to Love Your Leaver
Getting on With Your Life After the Breakup
Dwight Webb, Ph.D.
Softcover: $14.95   176 pages
Psychologist's sensitive, compassionate, insightful guide offers hope and encouragement to those in despair at the end of an intimate relationship.

Jigsaw Puzzle Family
The Stepkids' Guide to Fitting It Together
Cynthia MacGregor
Softcover: $12.95   120 pages
For kids wondering how the jigsaw puzzle pieces of their blended family will fit together. Engaging stories and gentle reassurance. Helpful suggestions for dealing with a new stepparent, new stepsiblings, new house, more.

Please see the following page for more books.

More Books With *IMPACT*